THE QUEEN

THE QUEEN

70 YEARS OF MAJESTIC STYLE

BETHAN HOLT

RYLAND PETERS & SMALL
LONDON • NEW YORK

Senior designer Toni Kay
Senior commissioning editor
 Annabel Morgan
Head of production Patricia Harrington
Art director Leslie Harrington
Publisher Cindy Richards

First published in 2022 by
Ryland Peters & Small
20–21 Jockey's Fields,
London WC1R 4BW
and
341 East 116th Street
New York, NY 10029
www.rylandpeters.com

ISBN 978-1-78879-427-5

A CIP record for this book is available
from the British Library.

Library of Congress CIP data has been
applied for.

Printed and bound in China

FSC
www.fsc.org

MIX
Paper from
responsible sources
FSC® C106563

CONTENTS

INTRODUCTION

The importance of the Queen's faultlessly appropriate style was crystallized within hours of her accession to the throne. Having flown back from a trip to Kenya in the wake of her father's death, the 25-year-old new sovereign waited inside the aircraft on the runway at London Airport while a black outfit was brought for her to change into before she was photographed for the first time as Queen Elizabeth II. Pinned to her left lapel as she descended the steps of the plane was her flame lily brooch, given to her during a tour to southern Africa with her parents and sister five years before – a small detail representing happy memories at a time of tragedy.

It is in this impeccable, considered vein that Her Majesty has continued for the last 70 years, the longest reign of any British monarch. The second Elizabethan age has seen the way women dress change almost beyond recognition – in the early 1950s, they rarely left the house without a hat and gloves, whereas now leisurewear and trainers can be the height of fashion. Trends for miniskirts, boob tubes, flares and power shoulders have come, gone, come back and gone again. The way fashion is consumed has changed, too, from genteel salon shows and homemade dresses to social media spectacles and shopping at the tap of a mobile phone screen.

Through it all, Elizabeth II's style has been an extension of all she represents as Queen; it is stoical and cautious yet dazzling and majestic. Five days after she ascended the throne, Prime Minister Winston Churchill called her 'a fair and youthful figure… the heir to all our traditions and glories'. It is testament to her success that, in her nineties, she is as revered for her singular style as she was adored for her beauty and youth in her twenties. No matter what is happening in the world, we can be sure that Elizabeth II will be there in her vibrant coat, her heirloom brooches and carrying her sturdy Launer handbag.

In 2016, in the year of her 90th birthday, the Queen received a special citation in *Vanity Fair* magazine's International Best-Dressed List. 'She has consistently represented who she is and what she stands for, without wavering from a standard she set a long time ago,' said Amy Fine Collins, the list's gatekeeper. 'Politics, culture, and class structure in the empire – all of that shifts constantly, but she doesn't. She's a beacon.'

In the past seven decades, it's estimated that Elizabeth II has worn more than 10,000 outfits, honing a clothing strategy that can see her semaphore respect, diplomatic flattery, elegance, gratitude, regal glamour and much more with what she chooses to wear.

And it's important to stress that choice – she is no star powered by an overbearing stylist. 'The Queen has a fantastic understanding of clothes and fashion, and is very aware of what suits her and what would be appropriate for the occasion,' her current dresser Angela Kelly has said. Hardy Amies, who designed for the Queen from the 1950s until the 1990s, emphasized that, 'I do not dress the Queen. The Queen dresses herself. We supply her with clothes – there is a difference'.

Rather than dismissing clothing as frivolous, Her Majesty knows just how much appearance counts. 'The Queen has a mind of her own. Just as she fell in love as a teenager and made a clear choice about who she wanted to marry, so she has decided how she should look,' says Justine Picardie, the author of *Miss Dior* and former editor-in-chief of *Harper's Bazaar*.

The Queen's image may be indisputably iconic now, but it is a style evolution that has not been without its challenges. The way she is seen by her subjects has been revolutionized from the black and white newsreels of post-war Britain and a generally deferential media to the technicolour 24/7 online news cycle that now exists, fuelled by tabloid outlets and technology that flashes an image or news line around the globe in seconds.

'The Queen must always present a perfect figure at all times – quite a high standard for any fabric and design to achieve,' Angela Kelly has said – a philosophy that she has evidently always sought to uphold but which must have extra urgency in today's media landscape.

Elizabeth II has grown from beautiful young woman to nonagenarian before the world's eyes, becoming a mother, grandmother and great-grandmother, and facing both joy and tragedy under that microscopic gaze. Reviews have not always been as glowing or respectful as they tend to be today, when most of us are in awe of the Queen's continuing dedication to duty.

One of her favoured designers, Ian Thomas, said that 'the Queen once told me she's no model girl and she doesn't want clothes to pose in', yet it must have been some ignominy to be accused of looking 'dowdy and tired' with 'visible veins' on her legs, as she was on one visit to Canada in her middle age. Who knows how Her Majesty took such criticism in private, but in public she has always seemed as keen to simply get on with the job when she's at her lowest publicity ebb as when she's at her most adored.

Naturally, the sovereign's style has evolved, with the subtlest of nods to changing fashion mores. There are outfits that she might rather forget but, overwhelmingly, as she prepares to mark her unprecedented Platinum Jubilee, there is no one in the world to rival her flawless, idiosyncratic look.

Genevieve James, who now runs her mother Cornelia James's eponymous glove makers, which has provided gloves for the Queen throughout her reign, describes the breathtaking impact that a meeting with the monarch at a Buckingham Palace fair for Royal Warrant holders had upon her: 'Everything went hush. I looked up and saw this small but rather alluring figure in the doorway. I realized that we were quite near the front and she was heading in our direction. She approached me, I bowed and said, "Your Majesty, I'm your glove maker." She laughed and said, "I know exactly who you are." The whole world fell away in front of me. She was wearing a beautiful bright green suit and she had fantastic skin; she was just sparkling. She's quite small in stature but she makes up for it; she's such a presence.'

That's the magic of Queen Elizabeth II.

PAGE 6 Queen Elizabeth II at Sandringham with her corgies, 1960s.

PAGE 6 Her Majesty wearing her classic brooch and triple-strand pearl necklace on a visit to Sweden, June 1956.

OPPOSITE At a polo match at Windsor Great Park, June 1976.

ABOVE The Queen and Duke of Edinburgh arrive at Baldonnel Airport, Dublin for a State Visit to Ireland, 2011.

from princess
TO QUEEN

When Princess Elizabeth Alexandra Mary of York was born on 21 April 1926, she was the first granddaughter of George V and a royal baby whose arrival was a cause for jubilation. Her grandmother Queen Mary wrote in her diary that Elizabeth's birth was 'such a relief and joy', describing her as 'a little darling with lovely complexion and pretty fair hair'.

There was every chance, then, that her father's elder brother and heir to the throne, Prince Edward, would go on to marry and have children of his own, and that Princess Elizabeth would be afforded a life of relative obscurity, perhaps as the horse-loving countrywoman so many perceive now as the 'real' Elizabeth. But the press knew all too well what might lie ahead; 'Queen of Hearts To-day, She may one day be Queen of England,' read the Pathé newsreel announcing her arrival, and when her parents visited Australia in the year after her birth, she was was declared 'the world's best-known baby', such was the feverish interest in the Duke and Duchess of York's daughter.

Even when she was tiny, Elizabeth's wardrobe was a topic of national fascination. It was revealed that her mother and both her grandmothers had sewn her layette themselves, with a little help from underprivileged women for whom it would have been a great honour to create clothing for

an infant princess. 'Many poor gentlewomen have profited by the Duchess's order for fine lawn and muslin frocks, little bonnets and jackets, and all the delightful accessories of baby's toilet,' read one report.

Meanwhile, the Duchess found herself at the centre of a debate about whether babies should be dressed in cotton or wool. Her own stance was clear; she declared that babies in wool looked like 'little gnomes' and that her own preference was for 'frilly babies' dressed in cotton. She set an example by rejecting anything too fussy, opting to dress her daughter, who soon took on the nickname Lilibet, in simple, sensible clothing rather than anything overly ornamental.

This stoical yet conscious attitude is one that would go on to shape Elizabeth's approach to style. In her controversial memoir, *The Little Princesses*, governess Marion Crawford observed an early lack of interest in clothing from the

future Queen: 'Lilibet never cared a fig. She wore what she was told without argument, apart from a long, drab mackintosh that she loathed.'

On 21 August 1930, Elizabeth's younger sister Princess Margaret was born and the close-knit York family was complete, famously calling themselves 'us four'. Despite a four-year age gap and the possibility of very different destinies, the sisters were soon declared trendsetters with their matching outfits, a deliberate strategy enacted by their parents to maintain as much normality and equality between their daughters as possible.

Photographs taken when Margaret was still a toddler show the girls in coordinating lace dresses and smart woollen riding coats. As they grew older, their outfits diversified into ruffle-trimmed floral frocks and kilt skirts with cardigans, a nod to their mother's Scottish heritage (see page 5). In 1932, social commentator Sylvia Mayfair declared that the Duchess of York was setting 'a Royal fashion lead that will undoubtedly be followed by many mothers'. Mayfair reported that she had spotted the 'two little princesses…

ABOVE H.R.H. The Duchess of York with her daughter Princess Elizabeth in June 1927.

driving in the park' where 'they were dressed in exactly similar raspberry sage coats with bonnets trimmed with rosebuds while neither wore gloves'.

The matching outfits were undoubtedly adorable and did their job of portraying Elizabeth and Margaret as two princesses in a pod. The historian Ben Pimlott described this time in their lives as a 'half royal existence'. But there could soon be no more pretending that the sisters were to come as a matchy-matchy pair forever, although the pretence of their coordinated outfits would continue well into their teens.

In January 1936, George V died and Edward VIII, Elizabeth's unmarried uncle, ascended the throne. The monarchy was thrown into crisis as Edward wrestled with an unsolvable dilemma – he must choose between his lover, the sharply chic, twice-divorced American socialite Wallis Simpson, and his duties as king. It was constitutionally impossible for the two to coexist.

In her book *The Royal Jewels*, Suzy Menkes describes the gulf between Wallis and the Duchess of York that was coming to represent the two sides of the crisis, and was as apparent in aesthetics as attitudes. 'As Mrs Simpson's blazing emeralds and rubies fuelled society gossip, the Duchess of York stuck discreetly to her strings of pearls and her domestic life,' Menkes writes, describing how the chintzy cosiness of the Yorks' home contrasted with the 'brittle sophistication' of Wallis's apartment.

On 11 December 1936, the King announced his abdication. 'I have found it impossible to carry the heavy burden of responsibility and to discharge my duties as king as I would wish to do without the help and support of the woman I love,' he told his subjects. Edward and Wallis became the Duke and Duchess of Windsor and were sent into exile in France. She was barred from using the styling of 'Her Royal Highness', although some would continue to address her in that way, including Nazi politicians during the couple's visit to Germany in 1937.

Edward's decision altered the course of the Yorks' life. The shy, nervous Duke became King George VI and Princess Elizabeth was now heiress presumptive; unless her parents produced a male heir, she would one day be Queen. The new King and his Queen Consort were now not only ruling over the United Kingdom, the Commonwealth and India, but they were also on a mission to return to the monarchy the reputation for stability, continuity and history that it had upheld since the reign of Queen Victoria until it was rocked by the abdication. In this mission, image was everything.

'The fashion context is so important after the disaster to the Crown of Wallis and Edward. The Windsors were held up as the epitome of chic by fashionable people, but in their traditional, matching outfits, Elizabeth and Margaret were their sartorial antidote,' says Justine Picardie.

The coronation of George VI and Elizabeth as King and Queen was the first opportunity that the new Royal family had to underscore their reliability and a particular brand of soft glamour that embodied history and regal grandeur. It was the King as much as his Queen Consort who understood this need to create a new perception of the Royal family. In his biography of the couturier Norman Hartnell – who would come to play a vital role in shaping the looks of Queen Elizabeth and later her daughter, Queen Elizabeth II – Michael Pick describes just how the designer was helped in his preparation for creating the coronation dresses for the Queen's maids of honour by the King as much as the Queen.

'The design of the Maids of Honours' dresses was discussed by both the King and the Queen with Norman, after they had together examined the painting *The Coronation of Queen Victoria* by Sir George Hayter and the King pointed out the headdresses of gilded wheat worn by the train-bearer,' writes Pick.

That afternoon, the King took Hartnell on a tour of the picture gallery and state apartments where they viewed 'paintings by Winterhalter, who endowed his women... with such regal and elegant grace... His Majesty made it clear in his quiet way that I should attempt to capture this picturesque grace in the dresses I was to design for the Queen,' Hartnell later recalled.

Although the honour of creating the Queen's coronation gown had gone to her long-time dressmaker Madame Handley-Seymour, it was evident that Hartnell had been chosen as the man to dress the family as they emerged onto the world stage. It was rumoured that the Queen had ordered up to 40 dresses from his coronation collection. She also entrusted the design of dresses for Princesses Elizabeth and Margaret, by then 11 and six years old, to Hartnell.

After the tumult of the previous year, the vision of the dignified new King, his bejewelled Queen in her dress embroidered with floral symbols of the nations over which they now reigned and their two adorable daughters in their bow-adorned dresses and little cloaks signalled a return to the calm dependability of the monarchy. This sense of steadiness was to become more cherished than ever as war loomed in Europe.

OPPOSITE The British Royal family in their coronation robes at Buckingham Palace after the coronation of King George VI on 12 May 1937.

In 1938, a tour to France was planned to establish the new King and Queen on the Continent. It was a visit with a three-pronged strategy: to introduce the new monarch and his consort, to cement the ties between France and Great Britain as the Nazis' ambitions to expand the German Empire became ever more urgent, and to subtly but surely remind everyone who the real royals were, as Edward and Wallis were making connections with some of the most influential people in French society. This was a charm offensive of the highest order.

'In addressing the Queen's image during his consultations, [Hartnell] now stressed both her soft femininity and small features; anything but the Parisian chic of Mrs Simpson,' writes Pick. The designer had been enlisted to create a wardrobe to wow the French for Queen Elizabeth, but just weeks before the tour, her mother died and the court was plunged into mourning. It was neither appropriate for the Queen Consort to wear black for the tour nor for it to be cancelled.

Hartnell looked to the history books for a solution. Taking inspiration from the medieval concept of *deuil blanc*, or white mourning, he remade all his creations in white. The couturier had remembered the viewing of the Winterhalter portraits that the King had given him the previous year, designing a series of gowns that revived the romance and femininity of the 19th-century crinoline. The reception of the Queen's wardrobe was rapturous; she was declared a fashion muse at home and abroad, rehabilitating her once-dowdy reputation. This twinkly, soft-as-marshmallow style would form the basis of the Queen's look for the rest of her life – and inspire her eldest daughter's attitude to clothing when she later began dressing for her own reign.

When war broke out in 1939, Princess Elizabeth and her sister were evacuated to Windsor Castle, while their parents mostly stayed in London, carrying out engagements to boost morale wherever they could. The family were careful not to seem ostentatious, surviving like everyone else on the rations they were allocated, but the Queen made an effort to dress in light, uplifting colours that signalled sympathy and optimism, another strategy Elizabeth would one day incorporate into her own wardrobe decisions.

At this point, Elizabeth and Margaret were still wearing matching outfits and the public's appetite for pictures of them was immense – and not only in Britain. In 1940, *Queen* magazine issued a plea for new photographs of the sisters: 'What the French women would like now are portraits of Princess Elizabeth and Princess Margaret, of whom they have heard so much... We have seen very little of the Princesses for such a long time that new pictures of them would be very much appreciated by everybody.'

Since the girls were small, their mother had chosen the photographer Lisa Sheridan to take occasional portraits of them. When Sheridan first encountered Princess Elizabeth, she described `her pretty doll-like face... framed in soft silky curls'. Much like the carefully choreographed pictures we see of Prince George, Princess Charlotte and Prince Louis today, these images gave people a glimpse of the royal children, but on the family's own terms. They were, in fact, a crucial tool in constructing a view of the Royal family as aspirational yet relatable and in touch.

A photograph taken by Sheridan at Windsor in June 1940 probably conjured everything the frightened nation needed to see from their little princesses; the girls look immaculately turned out in their pretty patterned frocks (matching, of course) with frilly Peter Pan collars and sensible Mary Jane shoes. While Princess Margaret plays with their corgi Jane, Elizabeth is engrossed in a book. There were few hints at the elder sister's impending womanhood, although for her 12th birthday, her mother had given her her first pair of silk stockings.

Just months after the Windsor picture, the Blitz began and the true ramifications of war became even more apparent. Although they were mostly closeted away, there were hints at the princesses' own contributions to the war effort and awareness of their own privilege; there were accounts of Elizabeth giving an old coat to an evacuee she met while on holiday in Scotland.

OPPOSITE Princess Elizabeth and her younger sister Princess Margaret Rose photographed by Lisa Sheridan at Windsor Castle in June 1940. With them is pet corgi Jane.

RIGHT Princess Elizabeth and Princess Margaret photographed by Dorothy Wilding in 1946.

It was the young teenager's equivalent of her mother's admission in September 1940 after Buckingham Palace had been hit by the Germans that she was 'glad we have been bombed. It makes me feel I can look the East End in the face.' A month later, Princess Elizabeth made her first radio broadcast on *Children's Hour*, offering her encouragement to her fellow evacuees. 'We are trying to do all we can to help our gallant sailors, soldiers and airmen, and we are trying, too, to bear our own share of the danger and sadness of war. We know, every one of us, that in the end all will be well,' she said.

Towards the end of the war, Elizabeth, now 18, began to carry out more public engagements, attracting adoration wherever she went. In early 1945, the future Queen made an even more practical contribution, joining the Auxiliary Territorial Service and training as a mechanic,

perhaps the only time in her life when she would routinely wear trousers and boiler suits.

Soon it was back to princess mode, however, as photographer Cecil Beaton – who had captured the Queen wearing her sparkling Norman Hartnell gowns in all their glory at Buckingham Palace before the war – was commissioned to take new portraits of Elizabeth (see page 11).

Beaton's recollection of preparation for the sitting reveals the thrifty attitude of the Royal family. 'I was bidden to the Palace to see the Princess's dresses, which were hung for display around the walls of her room,' he wrote. 'The most successful was the pink spangled crinoline that was one of her mother's pre-war dresses, now altered to fit the daughter.' For the first time, Elizabeth was shown as a glamorous young princess. Her journey to mastering the finer points of majestic style had begun.

In October 1946, Princess Elizabeth and Princess Margaret arrived at Romsey Abbey in Hampshire to act as bridesmaids for their third cousin, Patricia Mountbatten. When they entered the church, Elizabeth shrugged off her fur coat and handed it to the dashing naval officer usher, Philip Mountbatten, the bride's cousin. 'This small act jump-started a media frenzy, thanks to an air of ease and understanding between the pair,' Lady Pamela Hicks, Patricia's younger sister and later a lady-in-waiting to Queen Elizabeth II, remembered on her daughter India Hicks' podcast.

This was the first public hint of a love match that had been blossoming since Elizabeth had first met Philip on a visit to the Royal Naval College at Dartmouth when she was 13 years old. And despite the hopes of courtiers that the future Queen might fall for a rich Duke, it was the exiled and impoverished Prince of Greece and Denmark who stole the Princess's heart. And it was soon a matter of not if but when the couple would marry.

Elizabeth and Philip were persuaded to wait until after she had turned 21 to announce their engagement. Before that, 'us four' undertook a tour together to southern Africa, during which the Princess would celebrate her milestone birthday. Ahead of the family's departure, Queen Mary gave her granddaughter a pair of diamond and pearl earrings that she had herself inherited in 1897 (see page 161); the Princess would go on to wear them at her wedding 11 months later, but they were also a sign of the influence that the widowed Queen exerted on her son's heir.

The southern Africa trip might have been a last hurrah for the King's close family before Elizabeth married Philip, but it was also a rite of passage for her, not just in learning the ropes of the job but in dressing the part, too. The Queen and young Princesses had ordered a huge retinue of dresses for the three-month tour. In a press preview held by Norman Hartnell, there were 17 dresses for the Queen, 15 for Princess Elizabeth and 10 for Princess Margaret. Hartnell's fellow London couturier Captain Molyneux had made yet more outfits. In order to have enough fabric to make all these tour looks, some of the materials used were from dresses in the Queen's pre-war wardrobe. And there were off-duty clothes, too; Elizabeth and Margaret would ride together in the mornings wearing matching jodhpurs and shirts.

The family travelled 10,000 miles during the visit, which took place as Great Britain was in the grip of an unemployment crisis and crippling fuel shortages. Almost half of these miles were by rail,

ABOVE LEFT Princess Elizabeth speaks on the occasion of her 21st birthday on the 21 April 1947.

OPPOSITE Princess Elizabeth and Prince Philip at Buckingham Palace shortly before their wedding in 1947.

Princess Elizabeth and the Duke of Edinburgh photographed at Buckingham Palace after their wedding at Westminster Abbey, 20 November 1947.

with stories of the Royal Train stopping at villages where Elizabeth and Margaret would alight to greet people wearing their dressing gowns and jewels. They were lavished with gifts, particularly of diamonds, wherever they went.

It all sounds utterly luxurious, but when Elizabeth delivered her 21st birthday broadcast – in which she famously promised that 'my whole life whether it be long or short shall be devoted to your service and the service of our great imperial family to which we all belong' – she looked charmingly simple in a white silk dress, her only jewellery a double strand of pearls and a bangle.

The tour was an unmitigated success. 'They were modest, lovable, so anxious to please, so eagerly pleased,' wrote *The Spectator*, 'that it was almost painful to watch them doing their duty, and another duty, and still another duty, and a further duty, and anything anyone considered a duty – more, indeed, than was necessary for duty.' Duty was to define Elizabeth's life, but before she could continue her evolution as a queen-in-waiting, she needed her beloved by her side.

On 9 July 1947, the engagement of Princess Elizabeth and Lieutenant Philip Mountbatten was announced by Buckingham Palace. The couple posed for photographs, he wearing his naval uniform, she in a pale pink dress that had first been seen in South Africa. All the diamonds she had received there would surely have paled in significance compared to the ring given to her by Philip, which he had had made using stones from a tiara belonging to his mother, Princess Alice, who was by now living in Athens helping the sick and needy with no use for the jewels of her royal past. There is no mistaking Elizabeth's joy in these pictures taken with the man who would be by her side for the next 74 years.

THE WEDDING DRESS

The Chancellor Hugh Dalton described 1947 as an *annus horrendus* for the United Kingdom, which was still suffering the after-effects of the Second World War. The prospect of another winter might have looked even bleaker had it not been for a Royal wedding to buoy the nation's spirits. 'Austerity, coal crises, rationing and shortages faded from the news columns to make way for reports of the lovers,' wrote *Time* magazine.

At this moment, Princess Elizabeth's marriage to Philip Mountbatten was not only about sealing their love match but also represented the hope and promise of a new generation. Norman Hartnell turned to art as his starting point: 'I roamed the London art galleries in search of classic inspiration and fortunately found a Botticelli figure in clinging ivory silk, trailed with jasmine, smilax, syringa and small white rose-like blossoms,' he wrote. 'I thought these flora might be interpreted on a modern dress through the medium of white crystals and pearls.'

Translating the floral patterns of Botticelli's *Primavera* onto a gown proved to be an arduous process, and Hartnell wrote about his trials and tribulations getting the placements perfectly right. His head embroideress, Miss Flora Ballard, described how 'the motifs had to be assembled in a design proportioned like a florist's bouquet'.

It was perhaps inevitable that, in a world still politically fractured from conflict, the wedding gown would raise diplomatic questions; 10,000 seed pearls had to be sourced from America and were impounded by customs, while a row broke out about the origins of the silk being used for the dress – the press had to be assured that it had been made by Chinese worms from 'nationalist

LEFT The newly married couple make their way down the aisle of Westminster Abbey on their wedding day.

OPPOSITE Princess Elizabeth and Prince Philip leave the British Embassy in Paris during their four-day visit in May 1948.

China' rather than 'enemy' Japanese worms. The silk was produced at Lullingstone Castle, Kent and woven by Warner & Sons in Essex, while the duchesse satin was ordered from the firm of Wintherthur Silks, near Dunfermline.

Such was the public appetite for a spectacular gown that thousands sent in their ration coupons for Princess Elizabeth to use, although they were returned, as this would have been illegal. Instead, the Princess saved up her own coupons and the government gave her 200 extra.

In all, the wedding dress took 350 dressmakers seven weeks to create. It was stunning but understated, with a relatively modest 15 m/13-ft train, a sweetheart neckline and long sleeves. Hartnell's studio was deluged with press enquiries and the windows had to be whitewashed so that journalists couldn't snoop, though the couturier was said to be confident that his design was so intricate that it would be impossible to copy.

On 20 November, the Princess finally gave the world its glimpse of the much-anticipated gown as she arrived at Westminster Abbey, although the morning had not been without drama; Queen Mary's Fringe tiara, which had been loaned to Elizabeth by her mother, having been made by her grandmother from a necklace given to her by Queen Victoria, snapped just hours before the ceremony, and had to be taken to Garrard under police escort for repair. 'We have two hours and there are other tiaras,' Elizabeth's mother is reported to have said. Another courtier had been dispatched to fetch a pearl necklace that the Princess had decided to wear at the last minute.

'Her veil seemed as fine as cobwebs, her dress encrusted with crystals and pearls shimmered softly in the light of the lofty chandeliers,' read the *Telegraph*'s report of the day. Hartnell had done his job, crafting a moment of renaissance romance for a glamour-starved nation.

VISIT TO PARIS, MAY 1948

Within months of her marriage, Princess Elizabeth was expecting her first child. The world was unaware of this when she visited Paris with the Duke of Edinburgh (the title her husband had been given upon marriage by the King) in May 1948, and, despite battling morning sickness in unseasonably warm temperatures, succeeded in charming the French.

Norman Hartnell designed an 'elegant and suitable' wardrobe for Elizabeth, according to Pick, who concedes that there was 'nothing sensational' about the creations. For fashion watchers, this might have been a disappointment. Paris was still riding high from Christian Dior's revolutionary New Look collection, shown the previous year. The French designer had introduced an ultra-feminine silhouette that deployed yards of fabric to create voluminous skirts, while celebrating the female form with nipped-in, waisted jackets.

This exciting new way of dressing – which would go on to seduce Princess Margaret – had more to do with British royalty than you might think. 'It was the crinolines you designed for the Queen to wear in Paris in 1939 which inspired my evening dresses and the New Look,' Dior later told Hartnell. For the cautious – and pregnant – Elizabeth, embracing the New Look in Paris might have been a fashion step too far.

KENYA, FEBRUARY 1952

After two years spent in relative privacy, having her children Prince Charles and Princess Anne and spending long stretches of time in Malta, where Philip was stationed with the Royal Navy, Princess Elizabeth began to take on more royal duties in 1951 as her father's health faded.

She and the Duke remained a golden couple, renowned for their youthful good looks. Cecil Beaton sung the Princess's praises in the *Sunday Express* in July 1951: 'Princess Elizabeth's easy charm, like her mother's, does not carry across in her photographs, and each time one sees her, one is delighted to find how much more serene, magnetic and at the same time meltingly sympathetic she is than one had imagined,' he said. 'One misses, even in colour photographs, the effect of the dazzlingly fresh complexion, the clear regard from the glass-blue eyes, and the gentle, all-pervading sweetness of her smile.'

In October that year, Elizabeth and Philip visited Canada, where her wardrobe garnered huge praise, thanks in part to designs by Hardy Amies, who had refreshed her look with skirts 'just below the knee or certainly just above the calf' and the use of 'rich materials' because 'royalty should be dressed like royalty'. Such were the concerns for the King's health that mourning clothes had been packed for the Canada tour, but by the following February he seemed stronger, and it was decided that Elizabeth and Philip should set off on a long-planned tour of the Commonwealth.

En route to Australia, the royal party made a stop in Kenya for a safari holiday at a lodge called Treetops. Some reports suggest that at the moment when King George VI passed away in his sleep at

Sandringham, the new Queen Elizabeth II was wearing jeans as she enjoyed an encounter with a herd of elephants.

'We were the last people in the world to hear,' Lady Pamela Hicks, who was a lady-in-waiting on the tour, recalled. The rural location meant that news of the King's death was already being broadcast across the globe when the message reached Prince Philip, who took his wife into the garden, where they had been photographed standing on a bridge, to break the news that she was now Queen.

THE FUNERAL, FEBRUARY 1952

Back in Britain, the 25-year-old new Queen led her family in mourning. All were dressed according to strict dress codes, as set out during the reign of Queen Victoria – who shrouded herself in 'widow's weeds' for 40 years after the death of Prince Albert in 1861 – wearing only black and keeping jewellery to a minimum, then sticking only to pearls and diamonds.

There was still some generational disagreement about certain conventions, however. When Queen Elizabeth II arrived at Clarence House, she greeted Queen Mary – who was by now onto the sixth monarch of her lifetime – with a kiss on each cheek and a curtsy. Despite her advancing age and arthritis, Queen Mary curtseyed to her granddaughter, before switching quickly back to

grandmother mode. 'Lilibet, your skirts are much too short for mourning,' she admonished.

At her father's funeral on 15 February, Elizabeth, her mother and sister were shrouded in veils. Although her mother wore a skirt that reached to the floor, the new Queen's dress hovered above her ankles, a subtle but sure sign that this was a sovereign who knew her own mind.

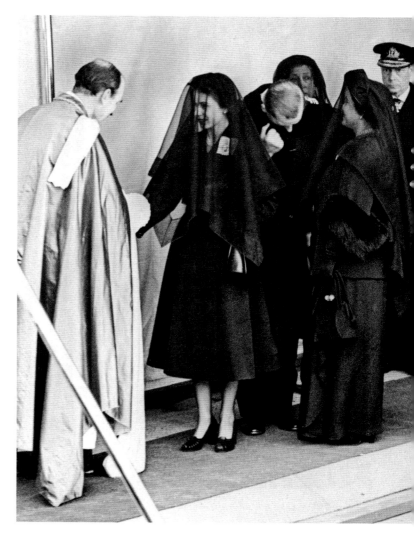

BELOW The Queen at the funeral of her father King George VI on 15 February 1952. Behind her can be seen her husband Prince Philip, the Queen Mother and the Duke of Windsor.

THE CORONATION GOWN

ABOVE Queen Elizabeth II seated in the Chair of Estate during her coronation on 2 June 1953.

RIGHT The Queen wearing the Robes of State in the Throne Room at Buckingham Palace on her coronation day. Her Maids of Honour are beside her and standing next to the Queen is her Mistress of the Robes.

In our current age of social media and rolling 24/7 news, the idea of an event breaking boundaries by being the first to be seen in grainy black and white footage by 277 million people around the world seems unfathomable. But Queen Elizabeth II's coronation on 2 June 1953 represented one of the first historic moments that could be witnessed in real time by so many. It's been estimated that an average of 17 people crowded around every television set broadcasting the BBC's coverage.

Eight months before, the Royal family's favoured couturier Norman Hartnell was asked to arrive a little early for a scheduled appointment at Buckingham Palace with Her Majesty. After years of loyal service, the Queen now honoured Hartnell with a unique commission – creating her coronation gown.

She asked for something similar to her wedding dress, in white satin but incorporating some colour, because she was by now a married mother of two. 'My mind was teeming with heraldic and floral ideas… everything heavenly that might be embroidered upon such a dress,' Hartnell wrote. His gown had to be both solemn and spectacular, a creation that would wow in photographs and on television screens, but also in front of the 8,000 guests in the Abbey.

He eventually sketched eight different designs of varying degrees of grandeur and presented them to the Queen. It was decided that instead of only incorporating emblems of the different nations of the United Kingdom, the gown's embroidery should represent all of the territories over which the Queen would now reign, an idea that would result in an intricate, scalloped pattern and shimmering palette of greens, pink and yellows achieved using silk threads, pearls, diamonds, amethysts, crystals and sequins.

It was this ninth design that Hartnell's seamstresses set about creating. The silk for the gown was produced at Lullingstone Castle, Kent

The emblems seen on the coronation gown

The Tudor rose for England

The thistle for Scotland

The leek for Wales

The shamrock for Ireland

Wattle for Australia

The maple leaf for Canada

The silver fern for New Zealand

Protea for South Africa

Lotus flowers for both India and Ceylon
 (now Sri Lanka)

Wheat, cotton and jute for Pakistan

And one four-leaved shamrock, added
 for luck without the Queen's knowledge

and was woven by Warner & Sons in Essex. It took nine weeks, six embroiderers and 3,000 hours to complete. To create the full-skirted shape, the dress was lined in taffeta and padded with three layers of horsehair crinoline, which made it incredibly warm and heavy – the Queen later said that it was akin to wearing a radiator.

In contrast to the sumptuous gown, Hartnell also made a strikingly simple linen dress that the Queen would wear for the anointing ceremony, a sacred moment that was not televised and saw Her Majesty remove all her jewels and her cape.

When the day of the coronation came, Hartnell was inside Westminster Abbey to proudly watch his designs make their debut upon the world stage. 'There was the dress I had worked on for months,' he later wrote, 'there it was shimmering and sparkling, its gold, its crystal, its diamonds and the muted colours of God's rainbow in the emblems that festooned her wide spreading skirt. Her Majesty told me graciously that the dress was triumphant.'

It's little wonder that Hartnell, who was appointed a Member of the Royal Victorian Order in recognition of his services to the new monarch and her family, was called 'the world's most envied dress designer' by the *Telegraph* thanks to his involvement in this spectacular event.

finding
A UNIFORM

Say 'Queen' today, and for almost anyone you ask, the image of
a lady wearing a brightly coloured coat, white gloves and block
heels, with a handbag perched on her arm and a brooch on her
left shoulder, will come to mind. But this was not the Queen
who charmed the world in the early 1950s.

Some elements, learned from her mother and
still firmly part of her style all these years
later, are familiar – the hats, gloves and jewellery.
But the nipped-in waists, experiments with floaty,
full skirts as much as slim-fitting pencils and
lustrous satin and lace materials are not.

'The Queen and Queen Mother do not want
to be fashion setters,' Norman Hartnell once said.
'That's left to other people with less important
work to do. Their clothes have to have a non-
sensational elegance.' Yet Elizabeth II did have
to negotiate the post-war fashion quake that
was underway as she shaped her Queenly image.

The sovereign's sister Princess Margaret was
busy forging a reputation for her fashionable
wardrobe. As a young girl, Margaret had said,
'When I am grown up, I shall dress like Aunt
Marina does.' Aunt Marina was the Duchess
of Kent, renowned for her chic clothes and
appearances in *Vogue* and *Tatler*. True to her

word, Margaret became a client of Christian Dior,
wearing one of his decadent tulle gowns for her
21st birthday in 1951, and kept up with trends
in a way her sister could not.

But Margaret did influence Elizabeth,
helping her to scout out new British designers
and introducing her to fresh names like Simone
Mirman, the milliner who went on to create some
of the Queen's most marvellous hats. Similarly,
the Queen would listen to her husband's thoughts
on outfits; many designers and milliners who have
made clothes for the Queen report that she would
use 'Philip doesn't like it' as an excuse for not
accepting a design.

Looking back at pictures of the Queen from
the 1950s with the rose-tinted glasses of nostalgia
though, she looks just as impeccably elegant as
Norman Hartnell described, beginning to shape
a look that was at once striking and sophisticated
but still appropriate to her role. When Christian

BELOW Queen
Elizabeth II and
Prince Philip
during their
Commonwealth
visit to Bermuda,
November 1953.

Dior showed a collection with skirts
40 cm/16 inches from the ground and
tops without corsetry ahead of Elizabeth
II's long-planned Commonwealth tour in
1953, the *Daily Sketch* newspaper
declared that there would be 'no Dior
hemline rubbish for the Queen when
she goes on her Commonwealth tour'.

Hartnell and Amies created between
100 and 150 outfits between them for
the tour, which would see the Queen
visit Bermuda, Jamaica, Fiji, Tonga, New
Zealand, Australia, the Cocos Islands,
Ceylon (now Sri Lanka), Aden (now part
of Yemen), Uganda, Malta and Gibraltar.
The reality of this tour was gruelling.
Elizabeth and Philip left their small
children at home for six months, and
on the Australian leg of the journey, the
party travelled an average of 370 km/230
miles each day.

But the images that survive from the
voyage look romantically glamorous; the
beautifully dressed young queen and her
handsome husband against all manner of
exciting backdrops. There is sumptuous
variety in Her Majesty's outfits. In
Bermuda, she wore a draped cotton
dress with a bird-like print, in Canberra
she wowed in a deep satin emerald skirt
suit and at a garden party in Sydney she
looked immaculate in a belted white lace
Hardy Amies dress (see page 31).

This era of Her Majesty's style
continues to inspire now; the stylist Mary
Fellowes revealed that it was her starting
point for a 'new fresh look' she gave to
Princesses Beatrice and Eugenie in 2012,
working with the milliner Stephen Jones
to emulate the neat, decorative hats the
Queen wore at this time. 'Granny gets the
reference. And loves it,' the Princesses
told Fellowes. Rachel Trevor-Morgan,
the Queen's milliner, also continues to
reference this period of the monarch's
style. 'If I look back at pictures or Pathé

The Queen and Prince Philip at a gathering of ex-servicemen and women in Canberra during the 1954 Royal Tour of Australia.

newsreels of the Queen, she wore such interesting hats; they were phenomenal,' she says. 'I find them inspirational for doing things now.'

Lady Pamela Hicks, the daughter of Lord Mountbatten who travelled with the Queen as her lady-in-waiting during the Commonwealth tour, remembers how conscious Her Majesty was of putting on a good show at home as well as abroad. 'There was a very nice moment arriving home when Queen Elizabeth (the Queen's mother) and Princess Margaret came on board as we tied up in London dock. The Queen is still in the dress she got up in. She looks rather smug as her mother and sister come aboard very smartly dressed indeed and she's just in her ordinary dress,'

remembered Lady Pamela on her daughter India Hicks' podcast. 'After lunch, as they're finishing their coffee, she disappears and comes back up in a completely new ensemble. As she came up she saw me looking and said, "I kept it for the return; I knew I needed to keep something back." '

Indeed, there are pictures of the Queen's triumphant return to London in May 1954, wearing a pretty peplum-waisted jacket and looking just as enchanting on Westminster Pier as she had in far-flung climes.

The Commonwealth tour was a masterclass in balancing elegance with duty. But the styles that the Queen wore so well could not be depended upon forever.

THE COPY-ME-QUEEN

It is often assumed that the phenomenon of dressing in the same clothes as our royals has only been possible since the Duchess of Cambridge decided to hit the high street for her regal wardrobe. There are few examples of royal fashions being accessible to the rest of us before that (even if copies were often produced by labels trying to cash in on the 'royal effect'), but there was a brief spell in the 1950s when women really could dress like the Queen.

This was thanks to her love of cotton dresses in dainty floral or abstract prints by Horrockses Fashions, a British ready-to-wear company established in 1946. The frocks were by no means cheap at between £4 and £7 each (the equivalent of an average week's wages), but they were so aspirational that women would save up to buy one for a special holiday or their honeymoon. They were ubiquitous in certain circles – one fashion editor reported counting 41 Horrockses dresses when she was holidaying in Madeira in 1953.

The dresses came to the Queen's attention when she was invited to choose some to wear during the Commonwealth tour to promote British manufacturing. Although the company offered to keep the styles chosen by the sovereign exclusive to her, she declined, simply asking that details not be released before she had worn them. This directive was a gift for the fashion pages; 'Copy Her Majesty, Her dresses are here' was just one of the headlines.

Reporters praised 'our Royal Family, who have done so much in their travels abroad to build up worldwide prestige of British fashions', and were now 'doing as much for the ready-to-wear industry as for haute couture'. The Queen continued to wear Horrockses dresses for warm weather tours throughout the 1950s, such as her visit to Nigeria in 1956. Fresh, pretty and accessible, the Queen's penchant for Horrockses is a forgotten highlight in her style evolution.

OPPOSITE Returning from her six-month Commonwealth tour, 15 May 1954.

RIGHT The Queen wearing a Horrockses Fashions dress on a Commonweath visit to Nigeria in 1956.

LEFT Queen Elizabeth II inspects flowers in the Palm House during a visit to the Royal Botanic Gardens in Kew, London, 1959.

OPPOSITE The Queen making the first trunk call on the Bristol Telephone Exchange in December 1958.

CREATING THE QUEEN'S FOREVER LOOK

There was a marked transformation in the Queen's style towards the end of the 1950s. The opulence and femininity of the decade shaped by Christian Dior's New Look began to give way to a sharper, sleeker and simpler silhouette as a new era dawned and Elizabeth II entered her thirties.

Not that she abandoned the aesthetic that had seen her through her first years as Queen entirely. In 1959, Her Majesty paid a visit to Kew Gardens wearing one of her prettiest-ever outfits, a lovely full-skirted lace dress with a coordinating bolero jacket and rose corsage in lieu of a brooch, even if it could have been from any point in the previous ten years. Yet just six months before she had been photographed wearing a fashion-forward leopard scarf, a style loved by stars like Elizabeth Taylor and Jayne Mansfield.

Although the sovereign was hardly wholeheartedly embracing the sweeping fashion changes suggested by beatniks, mods and the

avant-garde couturiers of Paris like Balenciaga and Givenchy, her silhouettes transformed – a detail that might have had as much to do with giving birth to her third child, Prince Andrew, in 1960 as keeping up with trends.

In November 1960, she wore a bright red skirt suit with a boxy jacket and straight skirt. Visiting Rome in 1961, she opted for a beautiful loose lilac duster coat, and at the inauguration of a memorial to John F Kennedy in 1965, her navy coat had a similar elegantly straight shape to Jacqueline Kennedy's two-piece.

As the sparkle of youth faded, the Queen was sometimes accused of looking 'dowdy, unfashionable and downright ugly', according to Michael Pick. And the trend for miniskirts was not taken up by a monarch with a strong instinct for the demure and respectable. 'You see, I was right not to shorten my skirts,' she would later remark once skirt lengths went below the knee again on the catwalks. Yet it was in this era that Her Majesty had found her look. Those bright colours and straight, smart silhouettes are what you think of if you close your eyes and bring the Queen to mind.

OPPOSITE Queen Elizabeth II and Prince Philip with Jackie Kennedy and her children, John Jr and Caroline, during the inauguration of Britain's Kennedy Memorial at Runnymede in May 1965.

ABOVE RIGHT The Queen on a visit in Kensington, London in November 1960.

RIGHT Queen Elizabeth II and Prince Philip, the Duke of Edinburgh touring the streets of Rome in an open-topped car during their 1961 trip to Italy.

THE QUEEN on tour

'Often we gathered in the Hartnell salon at night for news of what ball gown
the Queen was wearing on some far-flung Royal tour, yet he would not breathe
a word of it until the wire flashed through that she'd actually appeared in the
dress. Meantime, the champagne flowed, the jollity kept warm, the welcome
was always personal and kind'. These were the words of the *Telegraph's*
fashion editor Serena Sinclair, describing how reporters got their scoop
on the Queen's 'tourdrobes' in the earlier years of her reign.

There would have been quite a few nights like
this. Elizabeth II is the best-travelled monarch
in history, having undertaken almost 200 visits
during her reign to far-flung countries, ranging
from Norway to Nigeria, Panama to Portugal.
She has been called 'the million mile Queen'.

Her tours have ranged from one-day visits to
months-long excursions, where she's travelled by
plane, boat, train and car to cover as much ground
and greet as many people as possible – when the
Queen visited the USA in 1957, it was estimated
that a million Americans came out to see her.
Newspapers called her 'the Belle of New York'.

Clothing is an essential component in the
success of any tour. Always conscious of putting
on a good show, Elizabeth II and her entourage
put immense effort into ensuring she looks the

part day after day and night after night with
outfits that, at the very least, impress and,
hopefully, convey respect and soft power through
thoughtful colours and details.

'A huge amount of preparation is involved in
getting everything ready for any travelling, and
especially for a Royal Tour, from creating the
outfits and matching the hats, to making sure
the appropriate shoes, gloves and handbags are
selected and prepared,' Angela Kelly has said.
A ten-day tour might involve 30 outfit options,
allowing for changeable weather and unexpected
circumstances along the way.

Earlier in her reign, preparations were even
more monumental. On a 1959 tour to Canada, a
seamstress from Norman Hartnell accompanied
the sovereign, who was newly pregnant with

Prince Andrew, so that she could be assured that all her outfits would fit her changing shape. And when in 1977 she embarked on a two-month Silver Jubilee Tour to Western Samoa, Tonga, Fiji, New Zealand, Australia and Papua New Guinea, Her Majesty had four ladies-in-waiting to ensure everything was just so.

The Queen may appear effortlessly immaculate at all times, but behind the scenes it is a military operation to ensure standards never slip. The sovereign once travelled with enormous and cumbersome portable wardrobes, though she now prefers standard wheel-along suitcases. Acid-free tissue paper is used to prevent creasing and keep each garment pristine.

In a letter to Hardy Amies about an upcoming trip to South East Asia in 1972, Elizabeth II wrote: 'I find every time I read a programme for the Far East Tour, I get hotter and hotter at the prospect of six weeks in that climate.' To help alleviate some of these concerns, dessous-de-bras (detachable underarm pads used to absorb perspiration) were inserted into the Queen's dresses when appropriate.

But of course, the Queen's composure never belies any of these efforts. Wherever she is and whoever she's meeting, she never looks anything less than regal and cool. One tale from her 1977 visit to Fiji crystallizes this: when the roof of a building collapsed and panic ensued, Her Majesty simply took out her lipstick and reapplied it, the very definition of keeping calm and carrying on.

OPPOSITE Princess Elizabeth and Prince Philip seen at their most casual at a square dance party during their Royal Tour of Canada in October 1951.

CANADA, OCTOBER 1951

Just months before Princess Elizabeth ascended the throne, she and the Duke of Edinburgh made a much-anticipated visit to Canada, the first Royal Tour to the Commonwealth nation since the end of the Second World War. There was huge excitement and expectation surrounding the arrival of the glamorous young couple, with 4,500 journalists and photographers reportedly accredited to cover the month-long trip.

When the glamorous young heir to the throne and her dashing husband arrived in Ottawa, a local newspaper, the *Ottawa Evening Citizen*, described it as 'love at first sight' for the 'radiant and beautiful woman… the story-book princess come to life'. The *Globe and Mail* newspaper said there was 'that touch of fairy-tale atmosphere about her arrival'. Perhaps less fairy tale for Elizabeth was the reality of this intense interest; upon landing in Montreal, her fur coat is said to have become covered in shattered glass from the exploding flashbulbs of the photographers.

Although the tour included several ball-gown and tiara moments, the most enchanting image from the trip has to be a rare shot of the royal couple in relatively casual clothes for a square dance hosted by Viscount Alexander, Canada's Governor General, who had become enamoured with the dance form after seeing it at the Calgary Stampede. Suitable outfits were quickly sourced for Elizabeth and Philip by the Duke's valet – a brown checked shirt and blue dirndl skirt for her and a pair of jeans, a checked shirt and cowboy belt for him. The result is one of the most informal and charming photographs ever taken of the future queen and her husband.

AUSTRALIA, FEBRUARY 1954

Soon after her coronation, the Queen and the Duke of Edinburgh embarked on an ambitious seven-month tour of the Commonwealth, travelling 64,400 km/40,000 miles to greet as many of her new subjects as possible. They spent two months in Australia, the first time a reigning monarch had visited the country. Several special outfits paying tribute to the nation had been prepared incorporating its national colour, sunshine yellow, and its national flower, the wattle.

Her Majesty combined the two in a daytime look, worn to a children's rally in Canberra, comprising a belted cotton dress and floral headpiece (see page 40). Conveniently, she was presented with a bouquet of coordinating yellow flowers.

Norman Hartnell had also created a special gown for this leg of the trip in golden tulle with wattle embellishments. The Australian artist Sir William Dargie was commissioned to paint a portrait of the Queen wearing Hartnell's design and his painting now hangs in Parliament House, Canberra.

FRANCE, APRIL 1957

In her early tours to France, Elizabeth dazzled her hosts with her beautiful and carefully planned clothing choices. 'The prestige of British fashions [in Paris] has gone up sky high since Her Majesty's arrival,' noted the *Telegraph*'s style correspondent, Winefride Jackson.

In April 1957, two particular gowns wowed Parisians. A silver lace column dress was said to have caused 'gasps of surprise and then of admiration'. More traditional but no less striking was Hartnell's 'Flowers of the Fields of France' design, worn by Her Majesty for a gala ballet performance at the Paris Opera. Embroidered with bees – the symbol of Napoleon – and wild flowers, it was an exquisite example of fashion flattery. The Queen paired the dress with the Grand Duchess Vladimir tiara.

PAKISTAN, FEBRUARY 1961

Some of the most vivid photographs taken during the Queen's early reign were from her visit to Pakistan in 1961. When Princess Diana and the Duchess of Cambridge have visited the country in more recent decades, they have shown respect for its customs by dressing in the traditional shalwar kameez.

Her Majesty's first tour took place in a markedly different era, when the attitude was that the Queen should remain in her world-famous uniform – although there is footage showing her visiting mosques with her shoes covered.

The images show the Queen resplendent in sumptuous fabrics and work-of-art millinery. At a costume parade in Karachi, the similarities and differences between Her Majesty's style and that of the women she's with is thrown into glorious focus – in a gold slubbed silk tea-length dress, feathered hat, white heels and long white gloves, the Queen is wearing a glamorous example of her own signature style as she inspects the jewel-toned, traditional costume in front of her, while other women around are in equally vibrant saris. Back home, newspapers instructed readers on how to 'get the look', advertising hats similar to those worn by the Queen that could be bought for 32 shillings 11d (about £30 in today's money).

Once again, Hartnell made several gowns for the visit including a design with a white and emerald train, depicting the colours of Pakistan's flag, and another crinoline-style creation in pale blue decorated with embroidery that paid tribute to traditional Pakistani patterns.

ABOVE Queen Elizabeth II at a costume parade in Karachi on the Royal Tour to Pakistan, 1961.

OPPOSITE The Queen, wearing Norman Hartnell, and Prince Philip, Duke of Edinburgh meet with Pope John XXIII in the Vatican City, Rome in 1961.

THE VATICAN, MAY 1961

The Queen has visited the Vatican four times during her reign. For her first three papal audiences, in 1961, 1980 and 2000, she observed the formal protocol that stipulates that female monarchs or heads of state must wear black in the presence of the Pope. As BBC Vatican correspondent David Willey put it, 'When the Queen went to see the Pope when she was younger, she dressed up like the Spanish infanta.'

Norman Hartnell designed the black lace and tulle dress that Her Majesty wore for her meeting with Pope John XXIII in 1961. He also made a matching mantilla that was secured with Queen Alexandra's magnificent Kokoshnik tiara.

For her 1980 audience, Her Majesty wore a velvet and silk taffeta gown by Ian Thomas, although Hardy Amies had also made an outfit and there was some press confusion about which designer Her Majesty was wearing. Amies was told that his design had not been 'conventionally black enough' but 'would be perfect for wearing at private dinners whenever the Palace was in mourning'. Indeed, the Vatican visits are a handful of the very few times the Queen has worn black in public when not in mourning.

The exception to the Vatican's black dress code is the *Privilège du Blanc*, which is extended to the queens of select Catholic countries, who may wear white for audiences with the Pope.

JAPAN, MAY 1975

The Queen visited Japan in 1975. By this time, diplomatic fashion gestures were being enjoyed not only by those who saw Her Majesty in person but by everyone who saw the colour photographs that were beamed around the world.

Hardy Amies created many of the Queen's looks for the tour and was in the country at the time of her visit. In his autobiography *Still Here*, he recalls a meeting being interrupted so that the Queen's arrival in Tokyo could be watched on television. 'I had no idea what the Queen would be wearing, and it was therefore with surprise and delight that I saw her looking young, fashionable and regal in a pretty mauve silk coat of ours. "Imperial colours," said the Japanese, "How flattering to us!" I had no idea that mauve was an imperial colour, but I shouldn't be surprised if the Queen had known.'

Another standout was Norman Hartnell's flowing turquoise gown adorned with cherry blossom appliqué that the Queen wore to dinner at the Prime Minister's residence one evening. She also debuted a neatly tailored day coat and dress in the red and white shades of Japan's flag.

NEW ZEALAND, FEBRUARY 1977

Her Silver Jubilee year of 1977 was a very busy one for the Queen, so much so that designers who made her outfits for the countless engagements had to get everything ready the previous year as there would be so little time for fittings amidst the tours and celebrations.

In February, Her Majesty attended a Māori Festival in New Zealand where she was pictured wearing a korowai, a traditional feather cape, over her peach coat. The Cambridge pearl drop brooch can be glimpsed on the Queen's left shoulder (see page 158).

It is considered a great honour for a non-Māori to be given a korowai, which takes many months to make by hand. The Queen was first presented with hers during her 1954 visit to New Zealand. Prince Charles and the Duchess of Cornwall and Prince Harry and the Duchess of Sussex have also been given them during visits to the country since.

SAUDI ARABIA, FEBRUARY 1979

Throughout her reign, the Queen and other members of the Royal family have been deployed on 'charm offensives' to strategically important countries. Her Majesty's trip to the Middle East in 1979 was designed to enhance relations with nations that formed one of the UK's most significant export markets and were its source of oil.

A senior Foreign Office official told the *New York Times* that the Queen's mission was also 'to try to settle the nerves of the Arab rulers' after the Iranian Revolution of 1978. Against this high-stakes backdrop, it was important for the Queen's clothing to be pitch perfect and adhere to the area's custom of modest dressing. The double act of Hardy Amies and Frederick Fox created a series of covered-up looks for Her Majesty. Amies wrote that a turban 'with flowing ends' was inspired by a 'desert film' starring Marlene Dietrich.

Amies also revealed that the Queen's long dresses did not go to waste after this tour – they were shortened and worn by the Queen at Royal Ascot.

OPPOSITE ABOVE Queen Elizabeth II wears a mauve silk Hardy Amies suit in Tokyo during a State Visit to Japan in May 1975.

ABOVE Upon arrival in Saudi Arabia for a visit in February 1979, the Queen is greeted by King Khalid.

OPPOSITE BELOW The Queen, wearing a korowai, a traditional Māori feather cloak, during her Silver Jubilee Tour of New Zealand in February 1977.

AMERICA, FEBRUARY 1983

The Queen's style has always been subjected to the scrutiny of the press. Often the reviews have been glowing, but there have been times, too, when commentators were unafraid to hold back their criticism.

One such moment was Her Majesty's trip to California in 1983, which coincided with some of the worst weather the state had ever experienced. A visit that the royal dressmakers assumed would be full of sunny days turned out to be a battle against the wind and rain – so much so that the Queen and Prince Philip even had to abandon the Royal Yacht *Britannia* at one point and take up residence in a San Francisco hotel.

Several of the Queen's looks were derided by the press, including the navy and white Norman

ABOVE LEFT Queen Elizabeth II, in a Hardy Amies dress adorned with California poppies, and Nancy Reagan arrive for a concert during an official tour of the USA in 1983.

LEFT The Queen sporting her 'pearly queen' hat during her visit to San Diego, USA in 1983.

OPPOSITE Arriving in Edinburgh wearing Sandra Murray to open the new Scottish Parliament in July 1999.

Hartnell skirt suit and matching Simone Mirman baker boy hat that she wore to visit a US aircraft carrier in San Diego, which was dubbed her 'pearly queen' moment.

Norman Hartnell designer Annette Harvey commented, 'The Queen knows what she wants. No way can one influence her', explaining that the monarch had altered the outfit sketch a little. 'It was a beautiful hat; photographs do not show readers how it looked,' she added. Ironically, this witty look is now considered one of the most fun the Queen has worn, and it was perfectly matched to the uniforms of the US navy sailors she was photographed alongside.

A less risky choice was a Hardy Amies gown created for a Hollywood gala during the visit. The designer said that he recalled Norman Hartnell's designs for the Queen that incorporated significant flowers and came up with the idea of a dress adorned with California poppies.

'Suddenly there it was; the happy, glistening white and youthful-looking party dress that I had always hoped the Queen would choose to wear,' wrote Amies.

SCOTLAND, JULY 1999

While her role is intended to rise above politics, the Queen has found herself embroiled in the big issues of the day from time to time. And though Scotland is as much a home to her as England – royal summer holidays are spent on the Balmoral estate in Aberdeenshire and the Queen Mother's family were Scottish – she has become caught up in the debate around Scottish independence, too. Ahead of 2014's referendum, she said to a well-wisher outside Crathie Kirk, the church at Balmoral, 'Well, I hope people will think very

carefully about the future.' A statement that was interpreted as a boost for the No campaign, which went on to win.

Another pivotal moment for Scottish politics came in 1999 with the opening of the newly established Scottish Parliament after Tony Blair's Scottish devolution referendum in 1997. The Queen made a special effort to show her affection for Scotland with a specially commissioned outfit created by the Inverness-based designer Sandra Murray. Inspired by the Scottish landscape, Murray's design featured a dress and coat in the purple and green shades of thistle and heather. The outfit was accessorized with an Isle of Skye scarf handwoven on the island of Lewis – proof that diplomatic dressing works close to home, too.

CANADA, JUNE 2010

For her most recent visit to Canada, the Queen pulled out all the stops with an elegantly diplomatic wardrobe.

Meaningful embroidery played a central role. For a dinner in Toronto, Her Majesty wore a white lace gown embellished with a glittering array of maple leaves, Canada's national emblem, created using Swarovski crystals. 'When the Queen was seen at the State Banquet… the media went wild,' Angela Kelly later wrote. 'Everyone loved the design and that the leaves all had the correct number of points.'

Kelly also paid tribute to the 'beautiful beadwork' that features in the traditional clothing of the indigenous Mi'kmaq nation, members of which the Queen was due to meet in Nova Scotia. She asked their chief if they would design an embroidered pattern to feature on the collar and cuffs of the jacket that the Queen would wear at the reception. The result was a delicate series of scrolling designs that showcased the community's unique skills on the world stage.

On Canada Day, the Queen looked resplendent in a red dress and jacket topped off with a white and red hat to inspect a Guard of Honour outside the Canadian Parliament – a colour scheme that not only matched Canada's flag but also the tunics of the soldiers on parade. The look was finished with the maple leaf brooch her mother had received during her 1939 tour to Canada.

A year to the day later, the Duchess of Cambridge appeared in Canada wearing the same brooch with her own take on a red and white outfit.

LEFT The Queen and Canadian Prime Minister Stephen Harper at a dinner, Canada 2010.

OPPOSITE ABOVE Inspecting a Guard of Honour on the same tour.

OPPOSITE BELOW Irish President Mary McAleese, Queen Elizabeth II, Prince Philip, Duke of Edinburgh and Martin McAleese attend a State Dinner during the Queen's 2011 visit to Dublin, Ireland.

IRELAND, MAY 2011

The Queen's 2011 State Visit to Ireland was a carefully planned mission and the first visit by a British monarch since her grandfather George V in 1911. Since then, Ireland had proclaimed independence in 1916, and in 1921 the Irish Free State had been created. The ensuing years had been characterized by frequent unrest and often vicious conflict.

Almost a century on, Her Majesty set out to renew relations, using her clothes to emphasize that desire. She arrived in Dublin wearing an emerald green coat and hat. It's a look that Stewart Parvin picks out as one of his favourite creations for the sovereign.

'She arrived in a very simple jade green coat; it had just one detail, which was an incredible knot made out of the same double wool crepe fabric as the coat,' he explains. 'It has a printed silk dress underneath it. We'd lined the coat in the same print as the dress and there's a moment as she gets off the plane where it blows back to show that lining. It's wonderfully glamorous, understated and chic, yet it was a very important historical occasion.' (see page 9)

The *pièce de résistance* was the gown that Angela Kelly created for the State Dinner hosted by President Mary McAleese. Adorned with 2,091 silk shamrocks and accessorized with a harp brooch, it was the epitome of respectful dressing.

The *Irish Times* concluded that Ireland had been 'charmed' by the Queen's 'innovative' and 'ground-breaking' visit.

THE QUEEN'S year

The Queen's calendar runs like clockwork. On any given day of the year, you can hazard a guess as to where she might be – Sandringham from just before Christmas until early February, Scotland from mid-July to mid-September. In between, weekends are spent in Windsor and weekdays at Buckingham Palace, although in recent years the monarch has spent more time in Windsor due to a combination of the 2020 Coronavirus lockdowns and old age.

Planned around this calendar is an annual schedule of events that form the rhythm of the Queen's year and uphold traditions, some of which date back hundreds of years. Some speak to her official role as monarch, while others have emerged as important personal occasions that reflect the interests which Elizabeth II – the woman, rather than the sovereign – has fostered, along with her family, throughout her life. Many of them remind us of the ancient customs that shape what we expect from our royalty, while others give an often thrilling glimpse at their 'human' side and the Queen's very real relationships as a wife (now widow), mother, sister, grandmother and great-grandmother.

That we feel as familiar with the image of Queen Elizabeth seated upon the throne in the Houses of Parliament dressed in all her finest and most precious regalia as we do with the vision of her in a waterproof coat and headscarf watching her granddaughter Lady Louise Windsor compete in carriage driving competitions is testament to the finely tuned insights the public is offered into the Queen's annual routine.

EASTER

In 1952, the traditional Maundy Thursday service, where the sovereign gives out coins to people who have done good in their communities, became the Queen's first public appearance since ascending the throne.

Taking place on the Thursday before Easter, Her Majesty is often accompanied by other members of her family to the service, as in 1968, when Prince Charles and the Duke of Edinburgh also attended the Westminster Abbey event.

This look was an early example of the Queen's uniform in all its glory – from the coordinating peach hat and coat to the long-handled handbag. Only the fur collar would not be seen today.

Easter Sunday is always a happy occasion for the Queen, who celebrates at Windsor Castle with her family, making a public appearance for the morning service at St George's Chapel. Elizabeth II often nods to the promise of spring that this season heralds by choosing particularly uplifting colours and details. In 2007, she really got into the spirit of the occasion, opting for an exuberant rose-adorned hat that would have been a worthy contender in any Easter bonnet competition (see page 54).

EPSOM DERBY

Anyone who knows the Queen even a little will tell you that horses are her great love, so she takes huge pleasure from attending the races each year. One of her favourites is the Epsom Derby, which takes place on the first Saturday in June.

Her Majesty's look for the Epsom Derby in 1965 is typical of her ultra-elegant Sixties style – the mint silk cocoon coat hits just at the knee, which was about as mini as the Queen ever went – and a bubble cap-style hat, a nod to the Space Age look pioneered in Paris by designers like Paco Rabanne and André Courrèges. Later in the day, the Queen donned a pair of sunglasses so that she could better study the racing.

LEFT Arriving for the Maundy Thursday service at Westminster Abbey in 1968.

The Queen and Princess Anne have rarely partaken in overt attempts at mother-daughter dressing, but when they both arrived at the Epsom Derby in 1988 wearing almost exactly the same shades of yellow, it can't have been a mistake. Their shared colour palette that day seemed to echo their shared passion for horse racing as they watched in deep concentration, accompanied by the Queen's racing manager, the Earl of Carnarvon. The Queen's flower-trimmed beret is by Frederick Fox.

LEFT The Queen attending the Epsom Derby in June 1965.

ABOVE Queen Elizabeth II and Princess Anne watching the racing at the Epsom Derby in June 1988.

TOP LEFT The Queen and Prince Philip appear on the balcony with their baby son, Prince Edward, during Trooping the Colour, 13 June 1964.

ABOVE On the balcony with the Prince and Princess of Wales and Princes William and Harry for Trooping the Colour, 1988.

ABOVE RIGHT The British Royal family look out from the balcony of Buckingham Palace during the Trooping the Colour parade on 17 June 2017.

TROOPING THE COLOUR

Although the Queen's real birthday is in April, the occasion is officially celebrated on the second Saturday in June in the hope that this is when the weather will be at its best – and it often is!

The spectacular sovereign's birthday parade shows off the full pomp and circumstance of which the British military is capable. From 1952 until 1986, the Queen rode in the ceremony dressed in the magnificent crimson dress tunic of the Colonel-in-Chief of the Grenadier Guards. Created by Savile Row tailors Bernard Weatherill, Her Majesty's tunic was specially customized to allow her to ride side-saddle. One of her go-to Fifties milliners, Aage Thaarup, created a tricorn hat with the white regimental plume, known as a hackle, at the front – a feminine take on a traditionally masculine item.

After the parade, the Royal family appears on the balcony of Buckingham Palace, a moment that, over the years, has underscored the dynastic continuity of The Firm. One of the most powerful images ever taken at Trooping the Colour was the 1964 balcony shot showing the Queen in her full military regalia while cradling her baby son, Prince Edward – it's a photograph that epitomizes Elizabeth's unique balancing act, showing her as both monarch and mother.

By 1988, the Queen had stopped riding in Trooping the Colour and was a grandmother of four. She appeared on the balcony that year coordinating with Princess Diana in shades of blue, her Ian Thomas double-breasted coat accessorized with the Dorset bow brooch.

By 2017, there were many new faces on the balcony, including the Duchess of Cornwall, the Duchess of Cambridge, Prince George and Princess Charlotte. The Queen looked as delighted as ever to be surrounded by her family. However, her slightly subdued pale blue outfit – one she had worn several times previously – reflected a statement released on the morning of the event, where she acknowledged that the UK was 'united in our sadness' after recent tragedies, including the Manchester Arena bombing and the London Bridge attack.

Queen Elizabeth and the Queen Mother at Ascot for the Royal Hunt Cup, June 1960.

ROYAL ASCOT

The Royal family has a centuries-long association with the Royal Ascot race meeting, which takes place each June. With its strict dress code and reputation for millinery excellence, Royal Ascot is always one of the style highlights of the year in the UK.

The Queen's dedication to honouring a traditional way of dressing has arguably shaped Royal Ascot's fashion reputation; betting on the colour of Her Majesty's hat has become as hotly contested as punting on the horses. So much so that Angela Kelly has had to take special measures to ensure the shade cannot be predicted ahead of the Queen's appearance, after a suspicious £2,000 bet was once placed. After a meeting with bookmakers Paddy Power to discuss the incident, Kelly now lays out several options each morning during Royal Ascot week.

The Queen hasn't missed a Royal Ascot during her reign – apart from when the event took place behind closed doors in 2020 – but her Ascot look has evolved. In 1960, the 34-year-old monarch was ultra chic in her nipped-waist floral frock and wavy brimmed hat, but also dressed remarkably like her mother – note their matching triple-strand pearl necklaces, elbow-length white gloves, white court shoes and even the white frame handbag placed in the crook of their left arms.

1991's Royal Ascot was another fine example of the ostentatious headgear the Queen and her clan always showcase, from the Duchess of York's purple and green ensemble to Princess Margaret's feathered creation and Her Majesty's bow-adorned floral hat, created to match her dress.

In 2021, Her Majesty only attended one day of racing, but made it count, donning a mint coat and hat with fuschia accents by Angela Kelly.

ABOVE LEFT The Queen with her sister Princess Margaret and daughter-in-law the Duchess of York at 1991's Royal Ascot.

ABOVE The Queen attends Royal Ascot on 19 June 2021.

GARDEN PARTIES

The final presentation of debutantes took place in 1958 – Princess Margaret said that 'we had to put a stop to it… every tart in London was getting in'. Over time, this rather dated tradition was replaced with three garden parties at Buckingham Palace and another at the Palace of Holyroodhouse in Edinburgh, which have become an opportunity to invite thousands of members of the public into the Palace grounds and thank them for their service to society.

Attendees are carefully arranged in groups that members of the Royal family work their way around throughout the afternoon, while sandwiches, scones and tea are served.

Taking place in May and June, the Queen usually chooses particularly vibrant hues for these occasions so that she can be spotted from across the lawns. Although the weather is usually fine, the garden parties go ahead come rain or shine – in 2011, Her Majesty showed off one of her many Fulton umbrellas with a trim matched perfectly to her outfit. Angela Kelly replaced the Queen's usual dark umbrellas with this collection of clear options in the early 2000s, meaning not even a rain shower could obscure the sovereign from excited partygoers.

RIGHT The Queen sheltering from the rain while hosting a garden party in the gardens at Buckingham Palace on 19 July 2011.

THE ROYAL WINDSOR HORSE SHOW

The Royal Windsor Horse Show is one of the public events where the horse-mad royals look at their most happy and relaxed. They have been attending for decades and there's a truly intimate, family feel from the photographs that emerge.

It's evident in an informal 1968 shot just how at home Her Majesty is at the horse show. While she's as immaculately put together as ever in her tweed skirt suit, black gloves and emerald and cream headscarf, those practical wellington boots show she's ready to get muddy.

Equally charming was a 2016 appearance at the show where she was presented with a Tesco gift card after her horse won the Tattersalls RoR Thoroughbred Ridden Show Horse Championship. In her cardigan, quilted gilet and wellies, the Queen looks more countrywoman than monarch.

THE BRAEMAR GAMES

The Braemar Gathering is one of the finest examples of a highland games event and is held each September during the Queen's annual Balmoral break. Her attendance each year has become another annual touchpoint of her reign, dating back to the 1950s.

The dress code here is tartan all the way, and her Majesty and her family members have sported some spectacular looks over the years in an array of designs. This 1994 combination of Prince Philip in a Cameron of Erracht (modern) tartan kilt and the Queen wearing a punchy purple and red jacket (in a custom plaid pattern) epitomizes the unique Braemar style.

BELOW Queen Elizabeth II and Prince Philip attending the Braemar Gathering in Scotland, September 1994.

THE POLO

Another highlight of the royal summer has long been the polo matches in which three generations of princes have competed, with many taking place at Guard's Polo Club, a stone's throw from Windsor Castle.

The Queen has rarely gone entirely casual as a polo spectator, but there is nevertheless a more subtly personal feel to her outfits. The 1975 shot opposite captures one of the most sophisticated ever images of the Queen and Prince Philip together, he resplendent in his smart riding gear, she immaculate in a complementary blue floral dress and jacket with a bold navy trim.

Meanwhile, in 1985 the Queen beamed as Prince Charles kissed her hand after presenting him with a prize at the Cartier Queen's Cup (an event named in her honour), her pink dress adding to her radiance.

ABOVE Prince Charles kisses the hand of his mother, Queen Elizabeth II, after she presented him with a prize at the Cartier Queen's Cup in 1985.

The Queen and Prince Philip at the prestigious Guards Polo Club, Smiths Lawn, Windsor in 1975.

THE STATE OPENING OF PARLIAMENT

One of the Queen's central duties as monarch is to give the Queen's Speech at the State Opening of Parliament, which usually takes place each year at the beginning of the new parliamentary session or following a General Election. It is a ceremony steeped in history and tradition.

For decades, it was the only moment in the year when Her Majesty would be seen wearing the Imperial State Crown, along with the crimson velvet robe of state and a glittering gown.

In 1966, the Queen wore a beautiful peau de soie taffeta gown with crystal embellishments created by Norman Hartnell. While the design is undoubtedly spectacular, it might have faded into obscurity had it not been altered by Angela Kelly and Stewart Parvin for Princess Beatrice to wear on her wedding day in 2020.

In recent years, the Queen has more often opted to wear her uniform of a bright hat and coat to deliver her speech. In 2017, this dress code was chosen after Theresa May called a snap General Election, which meant the State Opening of Parliament took place during the month of June.

Her Majesty wore a cornflower blue brocade coat over a blue and yellow silk dress. A matching hat featured blue flowers with pistils made from yellow seed pearls. Social-media users instantly compared the hat to the European flag, noting the similar colours and composition, and the potential

ABOVE Queen Elizabeth II delivers the Queen's Speech during the State Opening of Parliament in the Houses of Parliament in London on 21 June 2017.

LEFT In the Imperial State Crown and a Norman Hartnell gown at the 1966 State Opening of Parliament.

meaning of this when Brexit had become such a contentious political topic. Was the Queen declaring a secret affinity with Remainers? Angela Kelly has insisted that, despite the careful consideration given to everything worn by the sovereign, this occasion 'was a coincidence but, boy, did it attract a lot of attention'. Given that Her Majesty's role requires her to remain politically neutral, it's just as well.

RIGHT The Queen, Prince Philip and the Duke of Gloucester at the Remembrance Day ceremony, 1952.

BELOW The Queen stands beside the grave of the Unknown Warrior in Westminster Abbey on Remembrance Sunday, 2020.

REMEMBRANCE SUNDAY

Remembrance Sunday has always been an especially poignant occasion for the Queen, who lost her uncle, the Duke of Kent, in an air crash in 1942.

Aside from periods of mourning, this is one of the only times that we see Her Majesty wearing black. For her first Remembrance Sunday as sovereign, in 1952, when the memory of war was still fresh in public consciousness, the Queen underscored the importance of honouring those who had given their lives in the war with a coat in a striking, military-like cut.

Fast forward 69 years and the UK was fighting a war of a different kind. Just as a second national lockdown to combat the COVID-19 pandemic was

beginning, the Queen attended a small private ceremony at Westminster Abbey to mark a century since the burial of the Unknown Warrior.

Emulating the tradition started by her mother, which sees royal brides place their

bouquets at the memorial, a replica of Her Majesty's wedding flowers was laid. The Queen struck a sombre figure with the addition of her black silk face covering – a distinctive accessory that will date the image for decades to come.

CHRISTMAS

The festive season is as much about duty as family celebration for the Queen, who has continued the tradition that began in 1932 of recording a Christmas broadcast for her subjects.

On the 25th anniversary of the message in 1957, Her Majesty took another step into the technological future by filming her speech for television as well as radio. There began a custom that continues to this day of the Queen donning a suitably celebratory dress for the recording; with its twist-detail bodice and opulent fabric, her 1957 frock was the perfect party dress.

On December 25 itself, the Royal family makes a public appearance to attend a morning church service. Until the late Eighties, Christmas was spent at Windsor, where an elegant coat and pillbox hat in Christmas red were worn for worship at St George's Chapel in 1980.

Angela Kelly ensures that the Queen's Christmas day look isn't too similar to anything she's worn in previous years, but does offer a nod to the celebratory spirit of the day. 'There is so much media coverage, with pictures sent all over the world, and I take a lot of care in designing Her Majesty's outfit,' Kelly wrote in *The Other Side of the Coin*.

The 2005 ensemble seen below – a coat by Karl-Ludwig Rehse with a hat by Philip Somerville – is a wonderful example of the Queen looking Christmassy without becoming too literal. Those fur cuffs – this was before real fur was replaced with faux in Her Majesty's wardrobe – add a sense of luxurious glamour, while the camel hue is fashionable yet unexpected for a style icon so known for her bright colours. It just happened to match beautifully with the coat worn by the young girl presenting the Queen with a posy.

LEFT Queen Elizabeth II receiving flowers after the Christmas Day church service at Sandringham Church, 2005.

RIGHT With the Right Reverend Michael Mann, Dean of Windsor, after the Christmas Day service at St George's Chapel, Windsor, 1988.

OPPOSITE The Queen sitting at her desk after giving her traditional Christmas Day television and radio broadcast in December 1957.

MILESTONE moments

The Queen has carried out countless engagements throughout her 70-year
reign, and while each one will have left a lasting impression on the people
she met, those who came out to see her and the causes to which she gave
her attention, many will ultimately fade from public memory.

But the past seven decades and more have also been characterized by significant moments that have acted as anchors in Her Majesty's time on the throne; milestone markers that mean celebration as well as, at times, tragedy or solemnity.

Sometimes they are deeply personal events that become, thanks to the Royal family's unique position in society, times of national emoting, whether joyful or mournful. Other times, these are occasions that trace the dots of history, recalling similar rituals that have been marked by previous monarchs or creating new ones in jubilation at Elizabeth II's incredibly long life and reign.

Clothes, as always, are integral to summing up the meaning of the occasions, whether it is the simple choice of an uplifting colour or more subtle messages that are imbued in outfits to enhance those links to history. What's certain is that the Queen is aware of the days that will live on in the history books and that these call for something particularly special in the wardrobe department.

DECEMBER 1948 – PRINCE CHARLES'S BIRTH

A year after her marriage, Princess Elizabeth gave birth to her first child and her heir, Prince Charles. The Cecil Beaton portrait released a few weeks after his arrival encapsulates the young mother's adoration for her baby boy. The *Illustrated London News* wrote: 'The photograph on this page of Princess Elizabeth and her son is not only one of the most charming ever taken, but one of the most radiant studies of a young mother with her baby son. No mother, whether of royal or humble birth, who treasures the first photograph of her child for the memories it bestirs, can look at it unmoved.'

The portrait also hints at the style signatures we still recognize today – a triple strand of pearls and a new brooch, a sweet basket of flowers design studded with rubies, sapphires and emeralds that was given to Elizabeth by her proud parents to mark Charles's birth. She has worn it many times since, including at Prince George's christening.

MAY 1960 – THE WEDDING OF PRINCESS MARGARET AND ANTONY ARMSTRONG-JONES

Thirteen years after her own wedding and days after the birth of her third child, Andrew, the engagement was announced between the Queen's younger sister Princess Margaret and society photographer Antony Armstrong-Jones.

Margaret adored fashion and was a true trendsetter, wearing a Christian Dior gown for her 21st birthday portraits. But for her wedding, which would be televised, she opted for Norman Hartnell – a safe pair of hands as the favoured couturier of her mother and sister. Hartnell took a radical route with his design, creating a wedding gown devoid of embellishments that *Women's Wear Daily* described as 'monastic'. Cleverly, it offered Margaret a unique look amid her sister's beloved embroideries.

Hartnell also designed the Queen's 'more elaborate', as *WWD* put it, wedding outfit, a floor-skimming turquoise gown. It was to be the final time she would adhere to this old-fashioned style custom at a wedding.

The Princess Elizabeth with
Prince Charles, December 1948.

OPPOSITE The Queen, the
Queen Mother and Prince Charles
arrive at the wedding of Princess
Margaret and Antony Armstrong-
Jones in May 1960.

JULY 1969 – PRINCE CHARLES'S INVESTITURE AS THE PRINCE OF WALES

The investiture of Prince Charles as the Prince of Wales was a moment that symbolized one of the central challenges of the Queen's reign: how to meld history with modernity. On this occasion, fashion played a vital role in achieving this finest of balances.

Norman Hartnell created a strikingly simple pale yellow shift dress and coat with stand-up collar in a recognizably Sixties style, while milliner Simone Mirman crafted an unusual Tudor-style cap covered entirely in pearls and bugle beads.

'That was a huge labour of love because everything was done by hand; it took hours and hours and hours,' remembers Mirman's daughter Sophie. Hartnell called it the Queen's 'medieval helmet', while Cecil Beaton wrote a letter of congratulations, saying that the hat was 'absolutely perfect for the setting'.

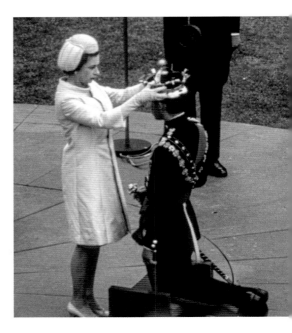

MAY 1972 – VISITING THE DUCHESS OF WINDSOR IN PARIS

The Queen and Wallis Simpson, the woman for whom Elizabeth's uncle King Edward VIII abdicated, were photographed together only a handful of times. The most notable was during Her Majesty's State Visit to France in 1972 when the Duke of Windsor, as he was known after relinquishing the throne, was nearing the end of his life.

Elizabeth, Philip and Charles visited the Windsors at their home in the Bois de Boulogne, Paris, posing outside with the Duchess. From a fashion perspective, it's fascinating to see these two women side by side. Both are undeniably style icons, but in completely different ways; whereas Wallis looks sharp and chic, with her hair in a chignon and wearing surrealist jewellery (much of it purchased from Cartier or Van Cleef & Arpels by her husband, an avant-garde antidote to the heirloom royal gems), Elizabeth II combines fashionable touches, like the graphic print of her Hardy Amies coat, with the hat, handbag and gloves that have been essential to her public look for decades and symbolize her stalwart dedication to traditional dressing – and her God-given role as Queen.

ABOVE RIGHT The Queen, in a Hardy Amies coat, stands beside the Duchess of Windsor on the steps to the Duke and Duchess's home in the Bois de Boulogne, Paris, May 1972.

NOVEMBER 1972 – SILVER WEDDING

For her silver, gold and platinum wedding anniversaries, the Queen chose outfits in corresponding colours. At a dinner celebrating 25 years of marriage to Prince Philip in 1972, Elizabeth wore a sleek column gown in glittering embroidered silver. Her decision to wear the State Diadem Crown, usually reserved for coronations and state openings of parliament, emphasized how intertwined she felt her marriage was to her job as monarch (see page 70).

JUNE 1977 – SILVER JUBILEE

'At nearly 51, the Queen is looking better than ever,' wrote the *Daily Telegraph* in a review of the looks worn by Her Majesty during the first part of her Silver Jubilee Tour to Australia and New Zealand.

Back in the UK, festivities continued with a public walkabout, Service of Thanksgiving and Buckingham Palace balcony appearance. It was an unseasonably chilly day. Royal couturier Hardy Amies wrote about his concerns that the original outfit he designed wouldn't have been warm enough. He was delighted, then, when Elizabeth appeared wearing another of his creations.

'The coat and dress were in an expensive pink silk crepe which we had lined in the same silk so that it was quite heavy. It behaved beautifully, even when the wind blew,' he wrote. The outfit came with a matching Simone Mirman hat featuring silk flowers – some reports suggest that the hat had 25 buds, one for each year of the Queen's reign, but that may have been wishful thinking, as the outfit had actually been seen already at the Montreal Olympics the previous year. If anything, the rewearing was a sign of Her Majesty's thrift and practicality.

There was another reason why she may have settled on that ensemble – as a young girl, Elizabeth had worn a similar shade for her grandfather George V's own Silver Jubilee, 42 years earlier.

ABOVE The Queen and Prince Philip, Duke of Edinburgh greet the public during a Silver Jubilee walkabout, 1977.

OPPOSITE On the Buckingham Palace balcony in an Ian Thomas coat and dress with the Prince and Princess of Wales following their London wedding in July 1981.

JULY 1981 – THE WEDDING OF PRINCE CHARLES AND LADY DIANA SPENCER

The fairy tale of Prince Charles and Lady Diana Spencer's wedding day was epitomized by the new Princess of Wales's voluminous silk taffeta gown, but Ian Thomas, one of the Queen's favourite couturiers of the time, ensured his client still stood out with a vivid turquoise coat and matching dress in the soft, flowing silhouette she favoured in the Seventies and Eighties. He also designed a turban-style hat decorated with silk

chiffon flowers at the back and sides to ensure a striking effect from all angles.

Unusually, the outfit was finished with a matching handbag, rather than the black or white leather styles Her Majesty usually carried. She also wore one of her most magnificent brooches, a floral style made using a stunning 23.6-carat pink diamond she had been given as a wedding gift by Canadian geologist Dr John Williamson.

AUGUST 1990 – THE QUEEN MOTHER'S 90TH BIRTHDAY

The tradition of the Royal family gathering together outside Clarence House each August to mark the Queen Mother's birthday became a wonderful opportunity to see them in public looking relaxed and happy together. This joy is expressed rather literally through the bright floral dresses worn by the Queen, Princess Margaret and Princess Diana for the occasion in 1990 when the Queen Mother turned 90. By blending in with her daughter-in-law and sister here, the Queen allows her mother a rare moment as the centre of attention in her pretty lilac outfit.

ABOVE The Queen, Princess Diana, the Queen Mother, Prince Charles and Princess Margaret on the Queen Mother's 90th birthday in August 1990.

OPPOSITE ABOVE RIGHT The Queen giving her *annus horribilis* speech at the Guildhall on the 40th anniversary of her ascension to the throne in 1992.

NOVEMBER 1992 – ANNUS HORRIBILIS SPEECH

One of the most famous phrases associated with Queen Elizabeth II is '*annus horribilis*', which she used to describe 1992. The year was 'not one which I shall look back [on] with undiluted pleasure', she said in a speech at the Guildhall, reflecting on the separation of the Duke and Duchess of York, the divorce of Princess Anne and Captain Mark Phillips and revelations about the state of the Prince and Princess of Wales' marriage, as well as a fire at Windsor Castle.

The Queen seemed to have dressed to match this gloomy assessment in a dark bottle green dress and velvet-trimmed hat. It was a rare departure from her usual palette of bright colours and a reflection of her sombre mood.

SEPTEMBER 1997 – PRINCESS DIANA'S FUNERAL

ABOVE Queen Elizabeth II standing outside Westminster Abbey at the funeral of Diana, Princess of Wales, September 1997.

The week between the death of Diana, Princess of Wales and her funeral was one of the most significant of the Queen's reign. During those seven days, Elizabeth had to wrestle with the opposing demands of her roles as grandmother and monarch, and readjust her behaviour to a new mood of profound grief and emotion. She faced anger for not having appeared in public for several days after the tragedy.

The Queen conformed to the strict mourning dress codes followed by the Royal family for the Princess's funeral at Westminster Abbey, at which she took the unprecedented decision to bow her head to Diana's coffin, wearing black tights and sticking to pearl and diamond jewellery.

Seeing the monarch in her mourning attire and hearing her speak to the nation 'as your Queen and as a grandmother' about her own struggles after the death of Prince William and Harry's mother went some way to repairing the fractures of the previous days. It was, perhaps, the very best test of the Queen's mantra that she must be seen to be believed.

JUNE 1999 – THE WEDDING OF PRINCE EDWARD AND SOPHIE RHYS-JONES

The Queen's youngest son opted to make his wedding ceremony an intimate family occasion, devoid of some of the usual traditions seen at royal weddings – there was no military presence and guests were asked to wear evening gowns and no hats. The Queen rose to the occasion in a striking lilac gown by Hardy Amies, formed from a knee-length embellished dress with a pleated chiffon skirt attached at the bottom. She couldn't resist adding a dramatic feathered headpiece, made by Frederick Fox, in lieu of a hat. The outfit was a spectacularly glamorous antidote to Her Majesty's familiar uniform.

RIGHT The Queen leaving St George's Chapel, Windsor with the father of the bride, Mr Rhys-Jones, at the wedding of Prince Edward to Sophie Rhys-Jones, June 1999.

NOVEMBER 2007 – DIAMOND WEDDING ANNIVERSARY

To mark their diamond wedding anniversary, the Queen and Prince Philip recreated the historic photograph that was taken of them as newly-weds enjoying their honeymoon at Earl Mountbatten's Hampshire country home, Broadlands. It wasn't only the linked-arms pose that the couple replicated – their outfits were similar, too. Elizabeth chose a skirt and jacket, accessorizing with strands of pearls and the same sapphire brooch – which had been given to Queen Victoria by Prince Albert – that she had worn in 1947.

OPPOSITE AND RIGHT The Queen and the Duke of Edinburgh celebrate their diamond wedding anniversary in 2007 (opposite). The location and their outfits hark back to a photograph of the couple (right) walking in the grounds of Broadlands on their honeymoon, 1947.

APRIL 2011 – THE WEDDING OF PRINCE WILLIAM AND CATHERINE MIDDLETON

Optimism and joy radiated from the outfit worn by the Queen to the wedding of the future king, Prince William, and his university sweetheart, Catherine Middleton. After a ten-year romance, Her Majesty's choice of colour and details seemed to symbolize the hope that this union gave for the future of the monarchy. Angela Kelly, the Queen's dresser, created the primrose yellow dress, matching coat and rose-adorned hat. She added beading and tucks around the neckline to create a sun-ray effect. With the eyes of a new generation on the Royal family that day, it marked a turning point in the Queen's popularity and status as a fashion icon – sales of Launer handbags shot up over 60 per cent after she was pictured carrying one at the ceremony.

Later that year, Her Majesty repurposed her wedding look as a diplomatic fashion statement when she wore the dress to church in Australia – where yellow is the national colour.

JUNE 2012 – DIAMOND JUBILEE RIVER PAGEANT

An impressive river pageant was held to commemorate the 60th anniversary of the Queen's ascension to the throne. The event was inspired by Canaletto's 1747 painting depicting Lord Mayor's Day, when the Thames was crowded with a flotilla of boats. Like Prince Charles's investiture, this was another moment when history and modernity came together to form a uniquely British spectacle. 'This was a unique occasion of a kind not seen since Tudor times,' wrote Angela Kelly.

The Queen's look for the day was a suitably elevated version of the sleek uniform that Kelly had by now established for her. In fact, she looked rather sparkling and diamond-like herself, in a design inspired by Elizabeth I, whose dress, according to the Royal Collection Trust, 'often featured white silks adorned with real jewels'.

The white tweed coat, a stark contrast to the red colour scheme of the Queen's barge *Spirit of Chartwell*, was woven with gold and silver thread, then embellished with diamantes for maximum sparkle. The frilled trim recalls Elizabeth I's extravagant ruffs, while the upturned brim of the hat ensured that Her Majesty's face was visible from the river banks. 'The overall effect suggested Britannia, the ruler of a maritime nation,' Kelly concluded.

JULY 2012 – THE OPENING CEREMONY OF THE LONDON 2012 OLYMPIC GAMES

Britain deployed two of its great cultural icons at the curtain-raiser for the 2012 Olympics, opening the Games with a sketch starring Daniel Craig as James Bond and the Queen as herself.

'She was very amused by the idea and agreed immediately,' wrote Angela Kelly in her book *The Other Side of the Coin* of the moment she told the Queen of director Danny Boyle's idea, which would involve stuntman Mark Sutton posing as Her Majesty parachuting into the ceremony.

'More than perhaps any other public appearance by Her Majesty, this would take meticulous planning,' Kelly continued, noting that she had to design a look which would stand out in the vast stadium but not in a colour that showed favour to any particular country, a hard task considering 204 nations were taking part.

Ultimately, Kelly settled on a peach dress with a pleated skirt designed to flutter as Sutton floated down from the helicopter, and the royal dressmakers created two identical versions of the dress – one for the Queen and another for Sutton.

BELOW LEFT The Queen, wearing an Angela Kelly dress, attends the Opening Ceremony of the London 2012 Olympic Games at the Olympic Stadium in July 2012.

FEBRUARY 2018 – LONDON FASHION WEEK

In her nineties, the Queen has become more of a fashion icon than ever, heading up a new generation of women for whom old age has brought respect and admiration. Grey hair and a traditional sense of style have become lauded, much emulated choices.

Elizabeth II cemented her treasured status among the world's fashionistas when she attended London Fashion Week in 2018 to present the inaugural Queen Elizabeth II Award to Richard Quinn, a Peckham-based designer best known for his bondage-inspired collections and only just out of Central Saint Martins.

'Once the models had walked out, they kept coming backstage screaming: 'That's the f------ Queen out there!' Quinn told me after the show, which the Queen attended with Angela Kelly.

True to form, she dressed in an impeccably sophisticated outfit for the occasion: a pale blue tweed dress and jacket with a slightly darker trim, pearl earrings and a diamond brooch. Her black gloves offered a stylish contrast to the light outfit. Kelly revealed that the look was 'modern but inspired by Chanel'. 'The colours and florals were her favourite part,' Quinn said.

American *Vogue* editor-in-chief Anna Wintour sat beside Her Majesty, but upset royalists when she failed to remove her trademark sunglasses. Perhaps the Queen didn't mind though? After all, if anyone knows the importance of dedication to one's personal style, it's Her Majesty.

ABOVE Queen Elizabeth II sits next to Anna Wintour as they view Richard Quinn's runway show before presenting him with the inaugural Queen Elizabeth II Award for British Design at London Fashion Week, 2018.

the designers
AND DRESSERS

Unlike the younger generation of royals, The Queen has not been a star-maker to a merry-go-round of designers and labels during her reign. She has always worn British, she has very rarely worn high street and she is best known for sticking to a highly exclusive set of names to whom she is fiercely loyal. This is as much a matter of practicality as anything; the demands on a sovereign's wardrobe are entirely unique and so bespoke clothing that can stand up to the rigours of royal life is a necessity.

Thus, instead of casting her sartorial net far and wide, Elizabeth II has depended on a close-knit team of designers and dressers whom she knows will help her to get it right with as little fuss as possible. By maintaining this small circle, the Queen also keeps control of her public image and the essential elements that have remained incredibly consistent over the years – if silhouettes were constantly changing or fresh upstarts were entering the fray with ambitions to try something new, the regal uniform recognized the world over would have been at risk of being diluted or confused.

The key players in this chapter are by no means an exhaustive list; there have been more aides in the Queen's coterie of dressers who have been indispensable at times during her reign, like Peggy Hoath, who was a member of the Royal household for more than 35 years after being seconded from Norman Hartnell in 1959. And the Queen's packed diary has meant that she has required multiple dressmakers to be working on pieces for her over the years – Alison Pordum, Maureen Rose and Sandra Murray, as well as Kenneth Fleetwood and Jon Moore during their time at Hardy Amies, are just a few of the names that have come up during my research.

But these are the characters who, across a reign spanning so many style eras, have guided the sovereign in first establishing, then gently evolving and cementing a signature style like no one else's, finely tailored to her singular position.

MARGARET 'BOBO' MACDONALD

The story of Margaret MacDonald, affectionately known as Bobo, is testament to the adherence to tradition and glacial pace of modernization that characterizes the Royal household.

Her relationship with Elizabeth began when the Princess was a baby; 'Bobo' was said to be one of the future Queen's first words, and she was thought to be the only person outside the family to call the Queen by her pet name, Lilibet.

Unlike the York girls' governess Marion Crawford, who betrayed the family's trust by writing a memoir of her time teaching the little girl who would go on to be Queen, Bobo was a faithful and discreet servant until her death.

As the Princess grew up and eventually ascended the throne, Bobo became her dresser and lady's maid, ensuring everything was just so and accompanying Elizabeth II everywhere, from her honeymoon to gruellingly long tours of the Commonwealth. 'Look after the Princess for me, Bobo,' King George VI told Bobo just days before his death as she set off for Kenya with Princess Elizabeth and the Duke of Edinburgh.

Bobo has been described as the 'scourge of milliners and couturiers', who feared her iron grip on the Queen's wardrobe and the strict rules she put in place, such as her insistence on certain types of handbag. Though many made attempts to give the Queen more stylish accessories as Christmas presents, they never saw the light of day.

Bobo made a brief appearance in the infamous 1969 documentary *Royal Family* (now banned from broadcast) showing the Mountbatten-Windsors behind closed doors for the first time.

In one scene, the sovereign and her servant look over sketches of outfits that they might commission for forthcoming engagements and Bobo is shown as a gentle yet firmly reassuring presence. 'Splendid, yes,' she says when the Queen picks one outfit. And when Her Majesty asks, 'Did I wear that one?' Bobo's instant reply is, 'No, that one's quite new.'

In her later years, Bobo was relieved of her duties and given her own suite at Buckingham Palace, which is where she died aged 89 in 1993.

NORMAN HARTNELL

Norman Hartnell's first design for the Queen was not her famous wedding dress or coronation gown, but a bridesmaid's dress that she wore to the marriage of the Duke and Duchess of Gloucester in 1935.

Three years later, he established himself as a designer worthy of elevating queens when he created the sensational 'white wardrobe' that Queen Elizabeth (the Queen's mother) wore on a tour to Paris in 1938. Inspired by the Winterhalter portraits in the Royal Collection, Hartnell established a soft, romantic look that launched the Queen as a style icon, even to the notoriously hard-to-please French (see page 15).

When he began designing for Princess Elizabeth, Hartnell imbued his creations with this same sense of classical beauty and symbolism. Though his meaningful references did have their limits; a row broke out during the design process of the coronation gown when Hartnell was told that leeks, rather than daffodils, were the correct emblem to represent Wales. 'I can't embroider a beautiful young woman's dress with leeks,' he protested, though he managed to make them look as lovely as English roses and Indian lotus flowers.

OPPOSITE ABOVE AND BELOW The Queen inspects a naval Guard of Honour at Auckland on her tour of New Zealand in December 1953 (above), and attends a reception hosted by the British Ambassador to France at the British Embassy in Paris on her tour of France in April 1957 (below), during the years she was dressed by her lady's maid Margaret MacDonald.

LEFT The Queen attending a film premiere wearing a white beaded evening gown by Norman Hartnell, 1960.

Glamour was Hartnell's speciality. It was said that his heart was never in a dress that could be worn before 5pm. 'I can't be bothered with those "who's for tennis?" dresses,' Hartnell once told the *Daily Telegraph*. At his height, in 1955, Hartnell employed 385 people and made 2,000 dresses a year for couture customers, including various members of the Royal family.

He was called 'Dear Mr Hartnell' by the Queen, who had immense affection for him; when he felt faint during one fitting, she fetched him a chair and insisted he sit down, despite her still standing, which is against protocol.

Although Hartnell had a sensitive appreciation for the significance of his designs and the diplomatic soft power they afforded the Queen, he could be snooty at times about the realities of how his clothes were worn. He loathed certain camera angles, like when Her Majesty was pictured bending to receive a posy wearing his creations.

In the 1977 Silver Jubilee Honours, Hartnell was made KCVO, a knighthood given in recognition of personal service to the Queen. He was declared 'the first fashion Knight', sealing his reputation as the man who arguably set the template for modern royal dressing, and one that still influences designers now.

Hartnell died in 1979, but you can still see the magnificent green marble facade of his headquarters on Bruton Street in Mayfair today, on the opposite side of the street to a plaque commemorating the birthplace of the Queen.

HARDY AMIES

It was in the midst of gloomy post-war London that Hardy Amies, who served with the British Army in Belgium during the conflict, established his own fashion house. During the 1930s, he had amassed a faithful coterie of clients during his time designing for Lachasse and, briefly, the House of Worth.

Amies revealed that it was his client Lady Alice Egerton who led him to Princess Elizabeth. When Alice became a lady-in-waiting to the Princess, the latter admired the former's clothes. Other sources suggest it was the Duke of Edinburgh who urged his wife to visit Amies after the clothes of the Hon. Sarah Ismay, another of Amies' clients, caught his eye. Eventually, the Princess made an appointment to visit Amies' salon with her sister Princess Margaret in 1950. It was to be the beginning of a working relationship that would last until 1990, with his label continuing to dress the Queen until 2002.

Amies' explanation of his reason for eventually stepping back exemplifies his famous acerbic streak. 'When I was 80, I said to my studio that an octogenarian can't go crawling around the Queen's tits, for God's sake,' he said in a 1997 interview, 'so I wrote to her and said, "Ma'am, I shall always be watching carefully what is going on but I think you should have the younger generation to wait on you." '

The designer's occasional disclosures about how he worked with the Queen

also suggest a yearning on his part to push the envelope a little more. He once said that the Queen is 'a bit frumpy', adding: 'If I suggest something to her, she will say firmly, "I don't want that Mr Amies, it's too chic for me." '

'I don't think she feels chic clothes are friendly,' Amies mused. 'The Queen's attitude is that she must always dress for the occasion ... There's always something cold and rather cruel about chic clothes, which she wants to avoid.' This was perhaps a jibe at the style of Wallis Simpson, famous for her cutting-edge wardrobe and exactly the image that Her Majesty would be seeking to avoid.

Despite these undercurrents, there was huge respect between Amies and the monarch. He was trusted with creating outfits for more than 50 foreign tours, gently moving her from the ladylike, New Look-inflected 1950s to the sleeker, simpler 1960s and beyond.

His finest moments touch on an impressive range of aesthetics, from a tiered crinoline gown worn at a reception during the Commonwealth Economic Conference in 1952 to a design inspired by the rococo interiors of the Schloss Brühl palaces in Germany in 1965 (the *Daily Express* described as 'a gown that stunned a nation') and the diaphanous gowns worn in the late 1970s. He was a dab hand at daywear, too – like the yellow polka dot dress, worn with a coordinating Frederick Fox turban that Her Majesty debuted in Mexico in 1975 (see page 87).

Amies was knighted in 1990, the year he stepped back from serving the Queen. When he died in 2003, Buckingham Palace said that Her Majesty was 'very sad' to hear of his passing; 'He contributed to her wardrobe over many years and she is, of course, saddened that he has died.'

IAN THOMAS

If Norman Hartnell and Hardy Amies set the foundation of the Queen's signature look, then it was Hartnell's protégé Ian Thomas who helped to modernize and refresh the monarch's wardrobe when he struck out on his own in 1969.

It was reported that when Thomas began his own company, he received a call from Margaret MacDonald. She said: 'Mr Thomas, the Queen wants to see you on Thursday afternoon at half-past two.' 'But what will Mr Hartnell say?' Thomas replied. 'It's not a question of what Mr Hartnell thinks. This is an order,' MacDonald replied. Thomas said that he was surprised that she knew about him: 'Ah, but we know so much more than you think.' You can almost imagine the wink.

Thomas encouraged the Queen to be a little more daring, coaxing her into soft, kaftan-like silhouettes for evening and tempting her to try the occasional trouser suit. He is said to have created a pair of lime green culottes that she wore in private.

'Instead of the hard, stiff satins, she now wears softer, more feminine chiffons,' he told the *Daily Telegraph*. 'We have even got her into evening separates. I prefer her in plain colours, but she does love prints. Of course, they do not show creases much.'

He also expressed some frustration at the conflicting demands of her role versus what might actually look best. 'I'd love to be able to design in darker colours for the Queen – she looks so marvellous in black – but she would simply get lost in the crowd,' he once said. He also grew to know the subtle signals that a design was not quite right; 'a raised eyebrow in the glass is all that it takes,' he observed.

BELOW LEFT The Queen, in a green floral evening dress by Ian Thomas, and Prince Philip entertain Sultan Qaboos on board the Royal Yacht *Britannia* during a State Visit to Oman in 1979.

BELOW RIGHT On a Royal Tour of Canada, July 1970, wearing a trouser suit designed by Ian Thomas.

Thomas, who also dressed Princess Anne and Margaret Thatcher, described how there would be corgis everywhere during his fittings with the monarch. A copy of *The World's Weather* was always handy so that the likely weather in whichever place they were preparing clothes for could be checked. He also said that the Queen would practice waving at herself in the mirror in each outfit.

The designer and his most prestigious client had a shared love of horses and corgis. She once allowed him to change a fitting time so that he could show his horse and her foal at the Horse of the Year Show, and the Queen sent her vet when one of his dogs was ill.

Thomas, who was made LVO (Lieutenant of the Royal Victorian Order) in 1977, died in 1993, leaving his home and possessions to the florist he visited each day to buy a flower for his buttonhole.

KARL-LUDWIG REHSE AND JOHN ANDERSON

German-born Karl-Ludwig Rehse had intended to build a fashion career in Paris, but when he made a brief visit to London in the mid-1960s, he met John Anderson, who was then working for the established fashion designer John Cavanagh.

The two men became partners in life and eventually in business. In 1988, they established John Anderson Couture and were invited by the Queen to show their collection to her at Windsor Castle. She ordered 16 outfits.

When she wore a blue and white look on a tour to Spain, King Juan Carlos said, 'Darling, you look wonderful.' It was a compliment that helped Rehse and Anderson to become firm favourites.

When John Anderson died in 1996, Rehse is said to have wanted to close the business but was persuaded by the Queen to continue. He reportedly enjoyed dressing her in her favourite shades of blue and apple green.

There might have been few major fashion 'hits' during this time, but Rehse always ensured that Her Majesty looked appropriate in well-tailored outfits. He admired her frugal insistence that she get maximum wear from her outfits, too.

Before his death in 2019, Rehse became President of the Royal Warrant Holders Association and he was made an honorary member of the Royal Victorian Order in 2015.

OPPOSITE LEFT Queen Elizabeth II wears a hat by Philip Somerville and a silk coat and dress by Karl-Ludwig Rehse to visit a housing estate on a trip to Singapore in 2006.

OPPOSITE RIGHT The Queen arriving at Newmarket in 1994 in an outfit by John Anderson.

RIGHT The Queen, wearing a coat and dress by John Anderson, with King Juan Carlos I of Spain on a Royal Visit in October 1988.

ANGELA KELLY

The Queen first met Angela Kelly in 1992 during a State Visit to Germany, where the Liverpudlian daughter of a crane driver and nurse was housekeeper to Sir Christopher Mallaby, the British Ambassador. The following year, she began work at the Palace.

It was the beginning of an exceptional relationship that has endured into the Queen's tenth decade and has helped seal her reputation as a style icon. Beyond ensuring Her Majesty looks immaculate at all times, Kelly has become a trusted confidante.

'The Queen is utterly charming all of the time,' Stewart Parvin told the *Telegraph*, 'but when Angela is there for a fitting, the Queen is noticeably more relaxed.' 'We have a lot of fun together,' Kelly once said. 'The Queen has a wicked sense of humour and is a great mimic. She can do all accents – including mine.'

Kelly has written fondly of her relationship with the Queen in two books, *Dressing the Queen: The Jubilee Wardrobe* and *The Other Side of the Coin*. Both titles offer a detailed look at Kelly's philosophy, which has been to update the Queen's outfits with more flattering cuts while also making use of the sumptuous fabrics gifted to the monarch over the years.

It's taken a steely attitude to get to her current position, and she has even confessed to acquiring the nickname AK47 among courtiers. 'I could not help thinking that the Queen's style needed to change quickly, before she was made to look

older than she was,' she wrote of her determined campaign to exert greater influence over Her Majesty's wardrobe.

It was a move that eventually led to her becoming one of only two designers who now dress the Queen, assisted by an in-house team of dressers, seamstresses and a milliner. 'It's been fascinating to see how Angela's guiding hand often tends towards a bolder, more glamorous look,' Parvin wrote in the foreword to *The Other Side of the Coin*. Kelly's official title is now Personal Assistant, Adviser and Curator to Her Majesty The Queen (Jewellery, Insignias and Wardrobe). In 2012, she was appointed LVO.

LEFT Wearing an Angela Kelly design, Queen Elizabeth II attends the Royal Variety Performance at the Royal Albert Hall, November 2012.

STEWART PARVIN

Stewart Parvin has been described as 'the most streetwise and down-to-earth dressmaker ever to have designed for the Queen'. It's perhaps not the most competitive field, but he has undoubtedly assisted Kelly in keeping the Queen's later-life wardrobe sharp and modern.

Kelly first scouted Parvin anonymously, following a recommendation from one of the Queen's ladies-in-waiting. She paid a visit to his shop and asked to take samples to show her employer. She was not only impressed with his design and tailoring skills, but the helpful reception she received.

The first dress the Queen wore by Parvin was a blue evening dress with an elegant sash detail for a State Banquet in Jamaica. Shortly before the event began, there was a power cut, so the dinner was lit by candlelight; the Queen's sparkling cobweb-patterned gown and diamond jewels twinkled beautifully.

'I go off and find as many prints, tweeds, colours, which aren't going to be easily available to other people, so they'll be in as small a quantity as possible so it is unique,' says Parvin of the starting point for his designs for the Queen. 'She needs bold colours because everyone wants her to stand out and, actually, she wants to stand out. She knows the significance [of her outfits] and that they're going to be on the cover of newspapers around the world, so she knows to make it pop.'

Parvin has also been entrusted with special commissions for the Queen's family members. He created Zara Phillips's wedding dress in 2011 and helped to alter the Queen's 1960s Norman Hartnell gown, which was worn by Princess Beatrice for her wedding in 2020 (see page 66).

The Queen made Parvin a member of the Victorian Order in 2016, wearing one of his dresses for the investiture ceremony. In 2020, Parvin rapidly switched from creating for the Queen to making scrubs for the NHS during the COVID-19 pandemic.

OPPOSITE ABOVE Royal dressmaker Angela Kelly seated beside Anna Wintour at London Fashion Week, February 2018.

RIGHT In Stewart Parvin at a State Banquet in Jamaica, 2002.

MAJESTIC glamour

The word 'Queen' still conjures a fairy-tale image of otherworldly glamour – a woman dripping in jewels and dressed in lavish gowns of the sort the rest of us can only dream of. Slowly but surely, Queen Elizabeth II has chipped away at those connotations with her unerring dedication to a slightly more functional daytime uniform, but she is all too aware of the vital importance of upholding the mystique. Thus, some of her most memorable outfits have been those that transform her into a magnificent, glittering vision of classic majesty.

'Of course, it's full of sequins – but you should just see how my duchesses lap them up,' Norman Hartnell said of one of his collections. Renowned for being most at ease when he was designing sparkling evening wear, the designer and young Elizabeth were a match made in heaven when it came to dreaming up the most regal gala looks imaginable. The couturier looked to the history books for inspiration, whether it was portraits of royalty through the centuries or references to different periods in court dress, like the 'robe de style' pannier look of the 17th century that provided the starting point for a gown worn by the Queen in 1963. Hartnell set the evening wear template for all the designers who have followed.

But the sovereign also recognizes the importance of moving with the times, and has not sought to channel regal fantasy for every evening engagement. These are also times when she's taken some of her biggest fashion risks, experimenting with boldly fashionable new silhouettes and eye-catching colours that you would never see in a Disney cartoon.

There are practical considerations, too. 'The Queen is happiest when her dresses have sleeves,' Hardy Amies wrote in his autobiography (a sentiment to which women the world over will relate). He also noted that the hems of evening gowns must be carefully considered to allow the monarch to walk easily. If only it *were* as easy as the swoosh of a fairy godmother's wand.

THE FASHION-FORWARD FIFTIES

The first decade of Her Majesty's reign was a time filled with experimental and trendsetting evening wear.

The first order that Princess Elizabeth placed with Hardy Amies was for clothes – including two evening dresses – for her first foreign tour with the Duke of Edinburgh in October 1951, to Canada. The white lace and gold gown that she wore at a State Banquet in Ottawa struck the perfect balance between classic and exciting, thanks to its full skirt and pleated 'cracker' neckline, drawing the eye upwards to her dazzling necklace and tiara.

Just months after ascending the throne, in October 1952, the Queen caused a sensation when she arrived at the Empire Theatre in Leicester Square for a royal viewing of the musical comedy *Because You're Mine*.

Pictures of a glamorous Elizabeth II wearing Norman Hartnell's black and white blazer-style gown appeared in almost every magazine and newspaper the following day, with manufacturers rushing

to make copies of the dress as quickly as possible. Even those on
a budget could emulate Her Majesty after a 30d paper pattern was
produced. The dress, dubbed the 'Magpie', was never worn again.

What to wear to meet one of Hollywood's most famous starlets?
This was the style dilemma faced by the Queen at 1956's Royal Film
Performance. Years later, Norman Hartnell recalled how he saved
the day with a somewhat unorthodox suggestion. Quizzed by the
Daily Telegraph about the questions most commonly asked of
him, Hartnell responded, ' "Why don't you put the Queen in black?"
Well, I did once. It was a grand first night with all the stars from
Hollywood in their baubles. I persuaded the Queen to wear black
velvet,' he remembered. 'Just a plain black dress. It was the greatest
triumph ever.'

Amid all the richly embellished and opulent designs that
Hartnell masterminded during his time serving the Queen, this
velvet number was one of the most successful, thanks to its
unusually stark simplicity.

THE SIXTIES *Old and New Collide*

The youthquake of the 1960s happened far from Palace walls, but the huge shifts that the movement created in fashion were thrown into sharp focus by the Queen's wardrobe choices.

Her gown for a State Dinner at the British Embassy in Tehran in March 1961 exhibited a finger on the pulse of evolving fashion attitudes. Instead of the usual fairy-tale designs, the Queen wore a chic, minimal, column-style dress that looked light and effortless, elegantly nodding to her hosts with intricate scalloped beading (see page 99). It was a look that seemed to show that the sovereign had an eye on the fashion pages.

Yet when America's young and glamorous new President and First Lady visited the UK a few months later in June 1961, it became not just a chance for two of the most iconic women of the 20th century to be photographed together for the first time but a clash of old and new style sensibilities; as a youthfully elegant new queen in the Fifties, Elizabeth represented that era's ladylike grandeur, while Jackie was carving a path as a new kind of power dresser, favouring Paris's latest clean, striking lines.

Although the Queen had been photographed in simpler, more column-like silhouettes – like the Tehran look – by this point, she opted for one of her most frou-frou gowns to host the Kennedys at Buckingham Palace: a blue tulle number in the crinoline style that Norman Hartnell had been using since the 1930s.

Jackie, on the other hand, was a vision of restrained elegance in an icy blue dress, which had been created by US boutique Chez Ninon as an 'interpretation' of a design originally by the pioneering Parisian couturier Hubert de Givenchy.

The President later wrote to the Queen, telling her that, 'we shall always cherish the memory of that delightful evening'. However, the Netflix TV show *The Crown* used the dinner as a tool to show the Queen feeling insecure and upstaged by the beautiful new First Lady. Jackie also reportedly told Cecil Beaton how unimpressed she had been by the Queen's style.

Meanwhile, Hardy Amies diplomatically pointed out that Jackie Kennedy and the Queen should have been beyond comparison: 'Journalists abroad would compare her [the First Lady's] appearance with that of the Queen's, forgetting totally that Mrs Kennedy was a president's wife and the Queen was a reigning queen.'

More than 60 years later, it's remarkable how both those looks have stood the test of time – neither would look out of place at a formal function today. And the Queen wasn't put off wearing the gown again – it was repeated in 1962 for a performance by the Scouts.

OPPOSITE The Queen and Prince Philip welcome President John F Kennedy and First Lady Jackie Kennedy to Buckingham Palace in June 1961.

THE BOLD SEVENTIES

The Queen's evening looks changed beyond recognition in the Seventies, in tune with evolving trends for brighter colours and more relaxed cuts. We might not think now of the monarch paying much attention to fashion, but she has always made her own efforts to stay relevant without being a slave to trends.

Designer Ian Thomas helped the Queen to craft a new evening-wear look, proposing graceful, flowing chiffons and splashy prints as a move on from the formal ball gowns of the past.

One of the most fabulous examples of this aesthetic is the orange and pink swirl-patterned gown that the Queen wore for the opening of the National Theatre in November 1976 (see page 4). With its dramatic bell sleeves and clashing colour palette, the kaftan design is typical of those worn by sophisticated women at the time. Princess Margaret attended the opening wearing a similar look, complete with cape.

Earlier that year, the Queen trialled another take on Seventies glam during a State Visit to Helsinki. Escorted by the Finnish President Urho Kekkonen, she wore a dazzling column dress covered in a glittering graphic design of green and gold sequins. It was a look that could have come straight off the catwalk of Studio 54 favourite, Halston.

THE EIGHTIES AND NINETIES
Playful Glamour

There was a witty touch to many of the evening looks worn by the Queen during the Eighties and Nineties. These examples remind us that Her Majesty has always been mindful of her freedom to make a statement with her wardrobe choices.

The festive season has always been a brilliant time for the Queen to have fun.

In December 1982, she attended a performance of the Royal Shakespeare Company's *Peter Pan* at the Barbican. Cleverly, her vibrant turquoise gown was finished with a ruffled Pierrot collar that gave a nod both to Elizabethan ruffs and the classic Peter Pan collar, so called after the costume worn by Maude Adams, who played Peter Pan in 1905.

In November 1999, the Queen wore one of her most famous evening dresses of all time at the Royal Variety Performance in Birmingham. Dubbed the 'Harlequin' dress, a gold chevron-striped skirt was topped with a sequinned, diamond-patterned bodice. The dress's creator Karl-Ludwig Rehse told the *Daily Telegraph* that he was 'overwhelmed' by the reaction to his design. 'People seemed to be thrilled at how she looked. She was stunning,' he said. 'She's like all ladies, she'll go for something new. She's fun to work with and very knowledgeable about fabrics. She knows how the clothes have to behave – how they have to move.'

OPPOSITE Queen Elizabeth II with President Urho Kekkonen during her State Visit to Finland in May 1976.

LEFT The Queen attends the Royal Variety Performance at the Birmingham Hippodrome in 1999.

ABOVE Arriving at a performance of the Royal Shakepeare Company's *Peter Pan* at the Barbican, London in December 1982.

STATE BANQUET CHIC

In recent years, the Queen's evening looks have tended to follow more of a formula – not that that makes them any less thoughtful or splendid. Her evening wear now appears designed to act as a backdrop to the veritable treasure trove of jewels that the Queen wears for formal evening occasions.

One exquisite example was the white silk dress with fine, powder blue embroidery that Her Majesty wore at the State Banquet for the King and Queen of Spain in 2017. The embroidery (and her aquamarine suite of jewellery) was cleverly chosen to match the Spanish Order of Carlos III, the most distinguished civil award in Spain, which was worn by both Queen Letizia and the Duke of Edinburgh. Letizia's vermillion red dress, meanwhile, matches Her Majesty's Spanish Order of the Golden Fleece. All in all, it's a masterclass in majestic splendour.

RIGHT The Queen and Prince Philip, the Duke of Edinburgh photographed with King Felipe VI and Queen Letizia of Spain before a State Banquet at Buckingham Palace in July 2017.

THE QUEEN of colour

The Queen has never given an interview, and when we do hear her voice, it is usually in scripted speeches, so we have few insights from the woman herself about her role. There is one illuminating quote, however, which has long been attributed to her. 'I can't wear beige because nobody will know who I am,' she once said, adding, 'I have to be seen to be believed.'

This is a seemingly simple observation, but one that shows acute awareness of her unique position, elevated above the rest of us and under some pressure to meet our expectations of what a Queen should be. It's an idea for which she has had to forge a new visual identity, in the same way that Elizabeth I had her power ruffs and Queen Victoria her opulent gowns and jewels. For Elizabeth II, the answer has been colour.

The Queen's daughter-in-law Sophie, Countess of Wessex elaborated on this strategy in the documentary *The Queen at 90*. 'She needs to stand out for people to be able to say "I saw the Queen",' she said. Standing at just 5ft 3ins, adding height with hats and emphasizing visibility with bright colours makes the monarch stand out in crowds where she might otherwise risk blending into the background.

'She's very lucky that lots of colours work for her,' observes Her Majesty's couturier Stewart Parvin. 'And she's not afraid to wear them. The Queen is small, so colour makes her stand out, particularly in a sea of men in suits.'

Since the earliest years of her reign, choosing vibrant, striking and meaningful hues has been a cornerstone of the Queen's look. 'For some time, the Queen, though she is not madly fond of clothes, has shown that she does have a decided taste in colours. Although pink and blue make an appearance occasionally, her preference is for yellows and greens, particularly lime shades,' read one newspaper report about Her Majesty's style in June 1959, going on to describe the turquoise tulle and primrose satin gowns that she had commissioned for a recent trip.

'The Queen is aware that colours have all sorts of symbolic associations and that they can reflect a variety of emotions – happiness, condolence or respect, for example. So helping the Queen put across her desired message by selecting the right colour and outfit gives me real satisfaction,' wrote Angela Kelly in her book *Dressing the Queen: The Jubilee Wardrobe*. While an outing may not necessitate a particular colour, thought will be given to what is most appropriate and the shades that stand out most against the backdrop.

Many women shy away from eye-catching colours, but the sovereign has never shown such qualms, happy to wear purple one day and lemon the next. When British *Vogue* analyzed a year in Her Majesty's wardrobe in 2012, they reported that she had worn blue 29 per cent of the time, 13 per cent floral, 11 per cent green, 11 per cent cream, 10 per cent purple, 4 per cent yellow, 4 per cent red, 4 per cent orange, 2 per cent black, 1 per cent checked and 1 per cent beige – a true rainbow of outfits.

NEON AT 90

It is as a nonagenarian that the Queen's reputation for daring use of colour has flourished. Rather than shying away from powerful shades, she has realized just how well she suits some of the zingiest out there.

Lime and neon green hues have become signatures of Her Majesty's since she turned 90 in 2016 – it's a colour she's worn for Royal Ascot, the wedding of Prince Harry to Meghan Markle and to welcome presidents on state visits, but two occasions stand out for the meaning that came with these vivid outfits.

For years, women across society have spoken about feeling 'invisible' as they age, and there was certainly a stereotype that getting older would mean dressing in muted outfits. The Queen blew away these assumptions with the outfit she chose for Trooping the Colour in the year of her 90th birthday celebrations, however.

LEFT On the balcony at Buckingham Palace during Trooping the Colour to mark the Queen's official 90th birthday, 11 June 2016.

entering her tenth decade, surrounded by her family, none of whom, notably, attempted to compete with her colourful statement.

It was a moment that sent the Queen viral on social media. The terms 'neon at ninety' and 'high-vis highness' began trending on Twitter. Later, it emerged that she had inspired many more women to adopt her love for neon green, with sales of the colour rising by 134 per cent at some retailers. It's a look which has taken on a feminist subtext because of the message of visibility and vibrancy that it embodies.

When Prince Harry married American actress Meghan Markle in 2018, huge efforts were made to give her a rapid induction to royal life. Less than a month after their wedding in Windsor, the Duchess of Sussex accompanied her new grandmother-in-law on a visit to the North West of England, where they attended the opening of the new Mersey Gateway Bridge.

Opting for a wool crepe and silk dress and coat by Stewart Parvin paired with a wool crepe hat by Rachel Trevor-Morgan in an unmistakably bold shade of green, Her Majesty ensured that she stood out from the crowd – a gesture that seemed to acknowledge not just her position as monarch but also her status as a matriarch

While that day was a lesson in the unique demands of royal engagements, Her Majesty also offered the new duchess an example in the possibilities of regal style messaging.

Their appearance coincided with the first anniversary of the Grenfell Tower fire, a disaster that killed 72 people and led to debates about inequality in British society. The Royal family had been showing its support for survivors with frequent visits to the projects supporting them – and Meghan herself would go on to help by collaborating on a cookbook to raise funds for the Hubb Community Kitchen that had brought women together.

The public had been encouraged to wear 'Green for Grenfell' that day, a shade that had been adopted to remember the victims and the continuing fight for justice. Her Majesty did exactly that, in a lime coat and hat. As she and Meghan observed a minute's silence during their visit, the Queen's fashion choice became a globally recognized symbol of her solidarity and sympathy.

LEFT The Queen and Meghan, Duchess of Sussex attend a ceremony to open the new Mersey Gateway Bridge, June 2018, in Widnes, England.

THE BEAUTIFUL BLUES

When Hardy Amies began designing for Princess Elizabeth in 1950, he said that his mission was to coax her out of the blue outfits that she had become prone to wearing: 'I also wanted to get away from the cliché of the pale blue dress; at the same time, blue was obviously going to be the Princess's great colour, dictated by those oversized blue eyes.'

Since then, the Queen has hugely expanded her palette beyond blue, but it is a shade to which she returns again and again – not only because it suits her but also because it is at once eye-catching and calming, representing wisdom, consistency and serenity.

Blue has long been a favourite shade for the clothing of upper-class children, so when Elizabeth II attended a polo match in Malta in 1954 – an island where she and the Duke of Edinburgh had spent many happy months away from the spotlight in the first years of their marriage, before she ascended the throne – it was touching that she opted to match little Prince Charles and Princess Anne in their double-breasted coats with a silk coat dress of her own. The whole Royal party coordinated beautifully with the glorious blue skies, too (see page 114).

In 1970, the Queen chose blue for another island stop-off, this time in Fiji. Her green and blue colour block shift dress is one of the shortest she has ever been pictured wearing, just grazing the top of her knees – a nod to the miniskirt trend of the time and a style with echoes of Yves Saint Laurent's era-defining 'Mondrian' dress. The shade of cyan in the sovereign's dress reflects an important colour in Fijian culture, representing the Pacific Ocean and the vital role it plays in

ABOVE Queen Elizabeth II on her arrival at Suva in Fiji, during a tour to mark the bicentenary of Captain James Cook's maiden voyage to Australia, March 1970.

island life; the colour was used for a new flag for the nation, adopted six months after this visit from Elizabeth II.

While Emerald Isle green is traditionally associated with Ireland, that could not be the only shade worn by the Queen for a visit to Northern Ireland in 2012. Noting that Her Majesty had a day of engagements planned at both Anglican and Catholic churches, Angela Kelly decided that a cornflower blue material would be the perfect 'soft hue' for the occasion. After glimpsing a collection of Wedgwood china in the corridors of Windsor Castle, she decided to recreate the famous white reliefs with fine white lace. So not only did the Queen's blue outfit provide a calming centrepoint for her religious engagements, it became a tribute to one of Britain's finest craft exports, too.

WONDERFUL IN WHITE

The Queen rarely wears white clothing for daytime – she even requested that her coronation gown contain shots of colour. But when it is used, it's a shade that can have a distinctive impact. Often it is chosen to give the monarch a 'literal' dressing moment, such as when she wore a white jacket at the White House in 2007.

One of the most charming examples of the Queen in white came on 2010's visit to Canada when she took part in the International Fleet Review to celebrate the 100th anniversary of the Canadian Navy. Her white coat and navy hat were a reverse of the navy uniforms and white caps of the sailors, so Her Majesty at once stood out and matched beautifully. The bow details on her outfit, repeated on her hat, sleeves and pockets, marked out her femininity and provided a playful touch. Naturally, the monarch had the ideal brooch to bring the look together – a sapphire and diamond design that had belonged to her mother.

NOT-SO-MELLOW YELLOW

Despite being a tricky shade to wear, yellow has been one of the flagship colours of the Queen's reign, chosen for many occasions. It tends to serve two purposes for Her Majesty: to show her loyalty to Australia or to project joy and happiness.

When Elizabeth II went Down Under in 1970, she took a new yellow coat and dress with a white trim by Norman Hartnell; an on-trend look that showed her gently moving with the times.

It was wearing this outfit that the Queen carried out her first ever walkabout, now a familiar sight on royal engagements, but then a revolutionary move in breaking down the barrier between the monarch and her subjects. What the Queen couldn't have planned was that one of the jockeys riding in the Queen Elizabeth Stakes at Randwick Racecourse, which she also watched that day, would have silks to match her outfit.

ABOVE Queen Elizabeth II attends a National Service of Thanksgiving as part of her 90th birthday celebrations at St Paul's Cathedral in June 2016.

ABOVE RIGHT The Queen chats with jockeys before the Queen Elizabeth Stakes at Randwick Racecourse near Sydney during a tour of Australia, April 1970.

OPPOSITE The Queen visiting the Red Cross headquarters on a tour of Switzerland in 1980.

Yellow is a colour that, almost literally, radiates optimism, a quality Angela Kelly has often taken advantage of in the past decade as the Queen has reached extraordinary milestones. One such occasion was the Service of Thanksgiving to mark her 90th birthday in 2016. Kelly created a coat, dress and coordinating hat for the occasion in a primrose fabric with delicate sprigs of white embroidery and scalloped edging, an outfit that spoke of vitality, contentment and celebration.

RESPLENDENT IN RED

There is no missing the Queen when she wears red, a colour denoting passion and regal splendour. It's a hue that she favours particularly during winter, when its warmth and festive connotations come into their own.

One of the most uplifting recent examples of this came in December 2020, when the UK was in the midst of soaring COVID-19 cases. The Royal family sought to be a beacon of hope and solidarity at this time, gathering outside Windsor Castle for a socially distanced reception thanking key workers and volunteers with carols played by the Salvation Army band. Conscious of the importance of the event, the Queen wore an outfit that was described as being 'Christmas red', accessorized with a candy cane striped scarf (see page 109).

On a visit to Switzerland in 1980, Her Majesty's scarlet outfit carried double meaning when she visited the headquarters of the Red Cross, whose symbol is an inversion of the red and white Swiss flag. With her red and white dress peeking out from under her bright red coat, the Queen's sartorial tribute was as obvious as they come, accentuated by photographs showing the neutral nation's flag behind her.

THE POWER OF PINK

Although she holds no political sway, the Queen is considered one of the world's most powerful women. Throughout her reign, she has been a woman in a man's world and has often found herself the only woman in a room full of men.

But the sovereign has never sought to emulate the men she's surrounded by, creating her own power dressing uniform grounded in emblems of femininity like handbags, gloves and dresses. Often she underscores her dedication to ladylike style by wearing pink, the girliest of hues, in the most masculine of settings.

When President Nixon made an informal visit to Buckingham Palace in February 1969, the Queen opted to wear a silk shift dress in the same shade of Shocking Pink popularized by couturière Elsa Schiaparelli in the 1930s. It was an unashamedly feminine and eye-catching choice, especially next to Nixon in his nondescript dark suit.

The sovereign achieved a similar sense of juxtaposition when she visited the Parachute Regiment of the British Army in 1990. Amid male soldiers in camouflage combats, she stood out in a rose pink coat by John Anderson. Her matching hat subtly echoed the berets worn by the servicemen, but apart from that, her outfit couldn't have been more different, marking her out as a figure of power in her own singular way.

OPPOSITE Queen Elizabeth II with US President Richard Nixon and followed by Princes Philip and Charles, 1969.

ABOVE The Queen inspects the troops of the 5th Airborne Brigade of the Parachute Regiment during a visit to Salisbury Plain in Wiltshire, England, May 1990.

MAUVE FOR MOURNING

Black may be a universally recognized colour of deep mourning, but Victorian codes suggested that another palette was suitable for half or second mourning, a middle ground between the austerity of black and a return to normality. This comprised shades of whites, greys and purples. While few abide by these rules now, they have offered guidance to the Queen in how she navigates dressing for more sombre engagements.

This was perhaps why both Elizabeth II and Princess Diana chose to wear lilac suits to the unveiling of a monument in Green Park in 1994 commemorating the contributions of Canadians to the victories in the First and Second World Wars. Black might have been too heavy, but lilac suggests respect, calm and contemplation. This was one of very few occasions when the Queen and another senior royal woman have worn the same colour at the same event.

There was a more personal reason for the Queen's decision to wear the same mauve outfit twice in the same month during the spring of 2021. After her husband of 73 years died on 9 April, Her Majesty entered a two-week period of mourning. She made a slow return to public duties afterwards, carrying out two of her most significant engagements of the year in early May and early June – the State Opening of Parliament and Trooping the Colour.

Her Majesty chose the same pale mauve outfit, originally worn to Royal Ascot in 2019, for both these events. Given how rare it is for her to repeat ensembles close together, this appeared to be a gesture that signalled that the sovereign was still in mourning, but an acknowledgment, too, of the public's expectation of seeing her wearing colour.

OPPOSITE Queen Elizabeth II attends a military parade, held by the Household Division, in the Quadrangle of Windsor Castle, to mark her official birthday on 12 June 2021.

ABOVE The Queen and Princess Diana in matching shades of lilac at the unveiling of the Canada Memorial Foundation Monument, London, 1994.

ALL THAT GLITTERS

Sumptuous metallic fabrics make only rare appearances in the Queen's style repertoire, but when they do, it makes for a sparkling fashion moment.

One such occasion was Her Majesty's visit to Slovakia and Slovenia in 2008. Angela Kelly described how her imagination ran wild when she learned that snow was likely during the visit: 'Immediately I felt inspired,' she wrote in *The Other Side of the Coin*. 'It was my first chance to design a winter wonderland wardrobe for the Queen.'

As well as creating a gown for the State Banquet from a 40-year-old piece of brocade fabric, Kelly designed a fur-trimmed white tweed coat and hat embellished with sequins, hoping that it would have the chance to twinkle against the snow-capped Tatra Mountains. Kelly was at pains to point out that the mink trim originally used on the coat has now been replaced with faux fur, a policy introduced in 2019.

In Australia in 2011, the Queen opted for a silver brocade jacket at a reception at Parliament House in Canberra. Earlier, Australian Prime Minister Julia Gillard had been admonished by the press for not curtseying to the sovereign and foregoing a hat when she greeted her at the airport. However, the two women were in accord at this event, both donning sparkling silver outfits.

OPPOSITE Queen Elizabeth II and President of Slovakia Ivan Gasparovic at Hrebienok Ski Resort on a tour of Slovakia in October, 2008 in Bratislava, Slovakia.

ABOVE The Queen, Prince Philip, the Duke of Edinburgh and Australian Prime Minister Julia Gillard attending an official reception at Parliament House in Canberra, Australia in October 2011.

LEFT Queen Elizabeth II visits The Eden Project, Cornwall during a G7 Summit in June 2021.

BELOW LEFT The Queen welcomes the Emir of Bahrain to a reception on the Royal Yacht *Britannia* during her State Visit to Bahrain in 1979.

OPPOSITE The Queen and Princess Anne photographed together, 1959.

FLORALS GALORE

When she's not wearing block colour, the Queen is most likely sporting florals. Ladylike, cheerful and classic, they have stood the test of time for Elizabeth II, forming a cornerstone of her wardrobe from childhood to today.

The pink patterned skirt suit worn by the monarch in a 1959 picture with Princess Anne is typical of the on-trend silhouettes she wore at the time. Posing beside a rose bush in full bloom, the photograph epitomizes Elizabeth II's consummate ability to dress to suit the occasion.

She was deploying the same skills 62 years later, when she attended an event at the Eden Project in Cornwall as part of the G7 Summit. In her painterly

pink and orange floral silk dress, the Queen coordinated impeccably with the attraction's rich variety of plant species.

Florals haven't always been a way to blend in, however. Like pink, they sometimes act as a beacon of femininity. There is perhaps no better image to sum this up than a portrait taken aboard the Royal Yacht *Britannia* during the Queen and Duke of Edinburgh's visit to the Middle East in 1979. Welcoming the Prime Minister of Bahrain, the Emir of Bahrain and his son Sheikh Hamad, the Queen's vivid neon pink and acid green floral gown contrasted spectacularly with her male guests' black and gold robes, ensuring that she stood out unmistakably.

the off-duty QUEEN

Fashion has undergone radical changes since the Queen was born in 1926 and her public style has, gently, reflected that. But from her childhood to her nineties, one aspect of Her Majesty's wardrobe has remained resolutely and remarkably the same: her off-duty country style.

There are photographs of a young Princess Elizabeth riding her pony in Windsor Great Park wearing a tweed jacket and jodhpurs and of her aged ten wearing a kilt and cardigan as she plays with one of her beloved corgis. These are exactly the kind of outfits that she has been pictured wearing in recent years, whether out for a ride in 2020, happily watching the Royal Windsor Horse Show in 2019 or relaxing with her great-grandchildren at Balmoral in 2018.

'For the Queen, the country is neither an idyll nor an escape, it is her real, royal world,' wrote Suzy Menkes in her 1992 book *Queen and Country*. Following the Royal family from Balmoral to Sandringham, she observes them hunting, shooting and taking tea, discovering that the Queen 'has a penchant for the Fair Isle sweaters sold in the knitwear shops in Ballater',

a town a few miles to the east of her Scottish estate. 'Wearing an old Burberry mackintosh, a headscarf, muddy rubber boots and wrapped up against the rarely kind Scottish weather' is how Stephen Barry, Prince Charles's former valet, describes Her Majesty's country attire to Menkes.

As much as glittering jewels or a rainbow of matching coats and hats, the off-duty Queen's twinsets and practical skirts are an instantly recognizable sign of a stoical approach to clothes (if it works, why change it?) and an unerring dedication to detail and heritage.

This is the look in which the Queen appears at her most relaxed and most like the horse-mad countrywoman she would have been had destiny not brought her to the throne. From silk headscarves to Barbour coats, Her Majesty has made rural chic style her own.

LEFT Queen Elizabeth II watches the Royal Windsor Horse Show International Driving Grand Prix in 1982.

ABOVE Watching the Carriage Driving event at the Royal Windsor Horse Show, May 1984.

OPPOSITE The Queen carrying her cameras and wearing a headscarf and Musto waterproof jacket at the Royal Windsor Horse Show, 1989.

COUNTRY STYLE

Great Britain is famed for its speciality in outdoor clothing – we do, after all, have a climate that can require sturdy footwear and rainproof outerwear year-round. For these businesses, the Queen has become one of their best advertisements.

Barbour was founded in South Shields in 1894 as manufacturer and importer of waxed cottons, and its classic jackets are still made in North East England today; Hunter was first established in 1856 in Edinburgh and went on to introduce its famous green rubber boots in 1956; in 1879, Thomas Burberry invented a hard-wearing yet comfortable-to-wear fabric called gabardine that would go on to be used to make the trench coats that would keep soldiers protected on the front line during the First World War.

These companies all began searching for solutions for protection against inclement weather, but the items for which they're now known have gained style kudos, thanks in part to having the Queen as a poster woman and the prestige of a Royal Warrant. Not that Her Majesty has set out to make these labels fashionable. She loves them because they do the job, whether she is spectating at the Badminton Horse Trials, inspecting her horses at Sandringham or deer stalking on the moors at Balmoral.

In 2012, Dame Margaret Barbour revealed that although the Queen would accept a new jacket as a gift to mark her Diamond Jubilee, her secretary insisted that the sovereign would also like her old coat re-waxed and returned to her. 'It's very desirable to have a very well-worn Barbour jacket,' Dame Margaret explained.

The monarch has also been seen wearing coats by Musto, which was granted a Royal Warrant in 2010 and counts Zara Philips, daughter of Princess Anne, among its ambassadors.

A crisp shirt or silk blouse paired with a neat cardigan are among the Queen's other countryside essentials. John Smedley and Pringle of Scotland are two more British labels with a Royal Warrant to provide the Queen with these wardrobe staples.

TARTAN AND KILTS

Acquired by the Royal family in 1852, Queen Victoria once called the Balmoral Estate 'my dear paradise in the Highlands'. Even today, the Castle provides a semblance of relaxation for the Queen and her family.

'Walks, picnics, dogs – a lot of dogs, there's always dogs – and people coming in and out all the time,' is how Princess Eugenie once described Balmoral life. 'It's a lovely base for Granny and Grandpa, for us to come and see them up there, where you just have room to breathe and run.'

Although the sovereign is never entirely on holiday, Balmoral is where she is at her most relaxed, and family days of walking, stalking, fishing and picnicking jostle alongside visits from the Prime Minister and other dignitaries. And as a photograph showing the Queen and Duke of Edinburgh smiling sat on the grass at the top of the Coyles of Muick released on the eve of Prince Philip's funeral in April 2021 revealed, a kilt is an essential element of Her Majesty's Balmoral uniform. The Queen has a wardrobe of kilt skirts in a huge variety of tartans, created for her by kiltmakers Kinloch Anderson who have been supplying the Royal family since 1903.

The Balmoral tartan was designed by Prince Albert in 1857 using shades of black, white and grey to reflect the Deeside granite from which the Castle is built. It is the Queen's personal tartan and can only be worn by others with her permission – the only person outside the Royal family who can wear Balmoral tartan is the Queen's piper, who traditionally plays for 15 minutes every morning at 9am outside her window while she's in residence in Scotland (see page 132).

Even when she's not at Balmoral, a plaid skirt denotes polish and practicality for Her Majesty. Paired with a shirt, cardigan and pair of brogues, plus an outdoor jacket if the weather requires it, this is her formula for country pursuits.

OPPOSITE BELOW
The Queen at the Royal Windsor Horse Show, 1991.

OPPOSITE ABOVE
With Princess Margaret at the Royal Windsor Horse Show in 1988 in a kilt and a matching lined jacket.

RIGHT The Queen with Prince Philip, the Duke of Edinburgh photographing a horse at the Badminton Horse Trials, 1973.

The Queen, wearing a Balmoral tartan kilt, confers the honour of Knight of the Order of Australia upon Sir Peter Cosgrove, the Governor-General of Australia at Balmoral, Scotland, August 2014.

RIDING

The Queen was put on a horse before she could even walk, the beginning of a lifelong passion that has endured well into her nineties. She is often pictured out riding in Windsor Great Park alongside her groom, still wearing the same riding attire that has been a signature since childhood.

Elizabeth II's equestrian look comprises traditional beige jodhpurs, a tweed jacket and chestnut leather riding boots, most often custom-made for her by Savile Row tailors Bernard Weatherill. Her Majesty usually chooses to eschew a riding hat in favour of a silk headscarf.

One of the most famous photographs of the Queen out riding was taken in June 1982 when Ronald Reagan and his wife Nancy became the first Presidential couple to be invited to stay overnight at Windsor Castle. During their visit, the monarch and US leader rode together. It was an image that came to symbolize the 'special relationship' between the two heads of state.

ABOVE Riding in Windsor Great Park with US President Ronald Reagan, June 1982.

THE HEADSCARF

A silk headscarf is one of the most iconic parts of Her Majesty's look. If she's not wearing a proper hat, then her carefully styled coiffure is usually protected by a delicately patterned scarf chosen to coordinate with the rest of her outfit.

When Gerald Bodmer, owner of Launer handbags, enquired about what Elizabeth II might like as a gift on her 95th birthday in 2021, her dressers gave a definitive answer. 'They said she would like a silk scarf with flowers measuring 86 x 86 cm/34 x 34 inches,' he says. 'I remembered that in 1990 I'd wanted Launer to start making silk scarves, so my wife and I had been to Como where Hermès' scarves are made. I sold most of them but remembered that I still had a few left, so I went to find them and realized they were the perfect size. I sent her two and received a very nice thank you from her lady-in-waiting.'

Having worn silk scarves since she was a teenager, the Queen's collection is undoubtedly vast. Over the years, she has been spotted sporting scarves bearing florals, graphic prints, rococo swirls, animals and offbeat sketches, often adding a subtly witty or decorative element to otherwise practical looks.

Many of the sovereign's headscarves are sourced from Hermès, making this one of the only elements of her wardrobe not to be routinely sourced from a British label. The French luxury maison, with its roots in exceptional equestrian craftsmanship, has been creating the crème de la crème of scarves since they were introduced by Robert Dumas (who also came up with the idea of naming the Kelly bag in Princess Grace of Monaco's honour) in 1937.

Hermès has often paid tribute to its association with Elizabeth II by issuing special designs in her honour. The first of these came in 1972, when legendary scarf and window designer Leila Menchari created the 'Regina' scarf bearing a painterly floral bouquet motif akin to the posies offered to the Queen during public engagements. The scarf, a favourite of Her Majesty's, has been reissued many times over the years in different colourways, including with a gold border to mark the Golden Jubilee in 2002.

In 1977, Menchari created another limited-edition scarf to commemorate the Silver Jubilee, bearing the monarch's elaborate coat of arms and motto 'Dieu et mon droit' (God and my right), while in 2016, the label marked Elizabeth II's 90th birthday by releasing a horse-themed scarf in tribute to her lifelong passion for horses, with £100 from every sale being donated to the Queen's Trust.

Besides Hermès, one of Her Majesty's most notable nonagenarian style moments came in December 2018 when she arrived at King's Lynn railway station in Norfolk to begin her Christmas break. Stepping off the train, she wore a camel coat – a contrast to her usual preference for vibrant colours – paired with a headscarf in the distinctive Burberry check. It was an outfit that had the fashion world in raptures.

OPPOSITE The Queen in a Burberry check headscarf at King's Lynn station in Norfolk on her way to Sandringham in December 2018.

ABOVE The Queen sporting a silk headscarf during the Badminton Horse Trials, April 1979.

SUNDRESSES

In 1956, Elizabeth II was photographed with a young Prince Charles watching a polo match in Windsor (see page 126). She appears to be attending as a wife rather than sovereign, dressed in a crisp cotton striped shirt dress that looks like one any of her subjects might have bought in a local dress shop or made from a pattern at home. Paired with lace-ups and a handbag, the only giveaways as to her regal status are that triple strand of pearls and distinctive set hair.

There are very few differences between this outfit and the one that the Queen chose for a visit to the ancient city of Petra in Jordan in 1984, almost 30 years later. Again looking more like a smartly dressed tourist than a royal, the monarch teamed a cotton shirt dress in an abstract pink and purple print with a matching cardigan and flat cream pumps. She carries a camera as well as her ever-present frame handbag, adding to the sightseer feel.

TROUSERS

OPPOSITE Queen
Elizabeth II and Prince
Philip, the Duke of
Edinburgh in casual attire
during a visit to the ancient
city of Petra on a Royal
Tour to Jordan, 1984.

ABOVE The Queen and
the Duke of Edinburgh
returning to the Royal
Yacht *Britannia* during
their Royal Tour of New
Zealand, March 1970.

The way the Queen dresses has altered only a little over the past 70 years, yet during her reign, the way women dress has transformed entirely. During Princess Elizabeth's childhood, trailblazers like Coco Chanel and Marlene Dietrich were defiantly showing that women could wear trousers and were becoming fashion muses because of it.

Like many women, Elizabeth had her first taste of wearing trousers during the Second World War, when she donned them in her job as a mechanic with the Auxillary Territorial Service, not as a fashion statement but as part of her practical khaki uniform. Once the conflict was over, skirts and dresses were reclaimed as symbols of femininity and grace (most famously by Christian Dior and his New Look), but trousers persisted as

The Queen and Prince Philip on safari during their State Visit to Zambia in 1979.

items women chose more routinely, especially when the likes of Audrey Hepburn and Marilyn Monroe popularized Capri pants.

Sightings of the Queen in trousers were few and far between, however, as she preferred to maintain the romantic view of the monarchy forged by her mother with her Norman Hartnell gowns and rose-tinted Cecil Beaton portraits.

Aside from a visit to a mine in Fife in 1958, where she gamely wore a protective boiler suit, the Queen wasn't pictured wearing trousers again until 1970 when she and Prince Philip took part in a re-enactment of Captain Cook's landing in New Zealand to mark the 200th anniversary of his historic achievement. For this engagement, Her Majesty wore one of her most casual outfits ever: dark slacks, plimsolls and a Harrington jacket.

Nine years later, the sovereign was seen wearing trousers again on safari in Zambia. Here, she looked elegant in beige pants and a gold, crimson and blue patterned cream silk blouse, finished off with a pair of sunglasses.

British newspapers had a field day in 2003 when Elizabeth II left hospital after a knee operation wearing a chic grey trouser suit. It was revealed to have been the creation of tailor Peter Enrione, who had been making clothing for the monarch since 1984. He said he had lost count of all the trousers he'd made for her, suggesting that the Queen enjoys wearing them in private.

'It's the equivalent of Prince Philip stepping out in a sarong,' one observer told the *Mirror*, while *The Times* noted that there had been 'an audible intake of breath' from onlookers when the Queen appeared. Since the mid-Noughties, the sovereign has left trouser-wearing to younger members of her family and is only seen in trousers when she's riding.

ABOVE The Queen leaves the King Edward VII hospital, London, wearing trousers and using a cane after a knee operation in January 2003.

the ACCESSORIES

'The Queen always carries her handbag and wears a hat; it's like her armour,' says Sophie Mirman, daughter of one of the Queen's best-loved milliners, Simone Mirman. 'The handbag is her shield and the hat is her helmet. It gives her that little bit of distance.' Indeed, the Queen simply wouldn't be the Queen without the accessories that have accompanied almost every outfit of her 70-year reign.

When her great-granddaughter Mia Tindall was pictured holding the Queen's Launer handbag aloft in a family portrait of the monarch and her two youngest grandchildren and five great-grandchildren taken to mark the Queen's 90th birthday in 2016, it was a sweet but knowing acknowledgment of one of the most important emblems of Her Majesty's life in the public eye.

If portraits of Elizabeth I incorporated globes to symbolize imperial power and a phoenix for longevity, the accessories seen in almost every image of Elizabeth II could be seen to deploy similar messages in a more modern way – her colourful and eye-catching hats are a beacon of her regal presence, her handbag is always by her side, just as she has promised that her 'whole life'

will be 'devoted' to 'service', and her gloves create an understated but absolute barrier between the sovereign and her subjects.

The Queen has shown remarkable restraint over the years, rarely veering from a simple but impactful set of accessories. It is perhaps only in her hats that imaginations have been allowed to run wild, with some rather flamboyant designs that have been permitted to nod to trends and add flair, though each one must still ultimately suit Her Majesty's requirements. But there have been no decadent heels, trophy bags or playful glove combinations; even for evening, there is a formula of gold or silver sandals with a small matching fabric bag. The Queen's accessories are as solid and dependable as the woman herself.

THE HANDBAG

Even before she became Queen, Elizabeth has never been without a sturdy frame handbag, which is seen hooked in the crook of her left elbow. When she visited Canada in 1951, just months before her accession, the Canadian author and journalist Pierre Berton observed her handbag trembling, the only sign of her anxiety as she embarked on her first foreign tour without her parents. 'Only an iron self-control hid her overwhelming nervousness,' recalled Berton.

If her handbag was the only giveaway to her nerves then, it is now synonymous with her public image, a symbol of steadfast dependability. When Her Majesty paid a State Visit to Italy in 2000, *La Repubblica* ran a front-page story with the headline, 'Ode to the Queen's handbag'. 'The secret of her regality is in that little royal but so ordinary accessory,' the article said.

The monarch's handbags have long been made by British firm Launer London, which was founded in the 1940s by Czech refugee Sam Launer. His bags soon became society and royal favourites. After a period of decline, the firm was rescued by businessman Gerald Bodmer in 1981 and he remains its passionate owner to this day.

'She's a sweetie,' he says of the Queen, whom he invited to visit the Launer factory in 1991, when it was based in London (manufacturing has since moved to Walsall, near Birmingham). 'We showed her how we made a bag from scratch and she was so interested she stayed for tea,' he remembers, adding, 'The Queen is totally aware of workmanship and totally aware of what's British – she said that to me.'

Bodmer remembers a somewhat tricky period before Angela Kelly arrived as the Queen's

ABOVE The Queen pays a visit to British Airways headquarters to mark their centenary year at Heathrow Airport in May 2019.

dresser, when it would be difficult for him to know the kinds of styles the sovereign would like. 'The Prince of Wales would give his mother a bag, then she wouldn't use it,' he says. Kelly brought some order to proceedings and 'got me to do bags which the Queen would like'.

The Queen's Launer handbags are made to specific requirements; they have an extra-long 40 cm/16-inch strap so that they hang comfortably from her arm, they are lined in silk and over the past eight or nine years they have been modified to be as light as possible for Her Majesty to carry.

Black calf is her favourite finish, although she does have bags in patent black, white and beige, and the Queen has not been tempted by Launer's rainbow offering of leathers. At a fair for Royal Warrant holders, when Elizabeth II noticed Launer's display of vibrant handbags, she asked Bodmer, somewhat incredulously, 'Do you really sell all those colours?'

Launer's handbags, which each take eight hours to create, are purposefully understated and devoid of bling, but each style is finished with a subtle yet distinctive gold loop logo. Bodmer is grateful that the Queen usually carries her bag with the emblem showing. 'It's very rare that she ever carries it the wrong way round. Years ago, her dresser told me to stick it on both sides but I didn't do that,' he confesses, keen not to take advantage of his VIP customer.

Although Launer has a long history of making bags for the Queen ('Since I've had the Warrant, I've never seen her with any other bag,' notes Bodmer), it was when she carried one at the wedding of Prince William and Catherine Middleton in 2011 that the label shot to global fame – its website crashed and sales shot up. Now bags, which cost upwards of £1,500 each, are bought online by customers around the world.

It's not just bags that Her Majesty purchases from Launer. 'The last thing she bought was five spectacle cases and she's bought purses in the past,' says Bodmer, who is also keen to clear up the myth that the Queen owns 200 bags, insisting that she only owns several styles in a few colourways. He won't be drawn on exact numbers.

The Queen's handbag is not just for show. She reportedly uses particular gestures to send messages to her courtiers. If she moves the handbag from one hand to the other, for example, it means that she would like to be moved along from her current conversation, while placing her handbag on the table means she'd like to leave in five minutes. A bag on the floor allegedly signifies that a more immediate getaway is desired.

One of the most Googled questions about the Queen is 'What's in her handbag?' A select few who have seen inside it at events report glimpsing a coin purse, lipstick, mints and sweeteners. She's also said to carry a portable hook that she can attach to a table to hold her handbag while she's sat down. When I ask Bodmer if he can shed any further light on the mystery, he replies, with a twinkle in his eye: 'Keep wondering!'

LEFT Queen Elizabeth II inspects the contents of her handbag while waiting for King Hassan during her State Visit to Morocco in October 1980.

THE SHOES

Of all her accessories, it is perhaps the Queen's shoes that have changed most markedly over the years. Of course, it hasn't been a radical shift, but there is a gentle yet discernable evolution from the fashionable peep-toe heels of the 1950s to the sturdy block heels she wears today.

Her Majesty is said to favour a heel height of 5 cm/2 inches – just enough to lend a sense of sophisticated elevation, but still perfectly walkable. The Queen's shoes are custom-made to fit her size four feet and Angela Kelly has revealed that she wears in new pairs for the sovereign so that she never risks rubbing or blisters – conveniently, the two women are the same shoe size.

Kelly also claims that familiar labels such as Stuart Weitzman, Carvela and Manolo Blahnik have been consulted about making shoes for Her Majesty, but mostly she now favours a chain-detail style by Anello & Davide (see page 141).

In 2018, a flurry of online stories suggested excitedly that the Queen might be a fan of Gucci's of-the-moment Horsebit loafers – in fact, her classic Anello & Davides simply bore a striking resemblance to the Italian design.

For many years, all the Queen's shoes were made by Rayne, a label that first began life as a creator of shoes for the stage in 1885. By 1935, the company had been granted its first Royal Warrant by Queen Mary. The royal relationship flourished, and it was later entrusted with making Elizabeth II's wedding and coronation shoes. The coronation shoes were designed by Roger Vivier, who would go on to establish his own label in France that reproduced a new version of the gold, fleur-de-lys-inspired coronation sandals in 2020, priced at £1,425.

Edward Rayne, who was knighted in 1988, would visit the Queen up to six times a year and was often asked to repair shoes – the sovereign's footwear often fell victim to damage from mischievous corgis – as well as create new ones. This relationship endured despite a rocky beginning to Edward's relations with Buckingham Palace; during a trip to New York in 1950, he was lavished with drinks by a journalist determined to discover Elizabeth's shoe size, which he eventually revealed to the horror of courtiers.

When Rayne ceased trading, palace staff tracked down cordwainer David Hyatt (who had been responsible for making the Queen's shoes at Rayne) at his new employers Anello & Davide, which was awarded the Royal Warrant in 2001.

As with many other aspects of the Queen's wardrobe, her shoes are rooted in sensible practicality but are also considered almost accidentally chic.

THE GLOVES

'Often people pick up on every aspect of the Queen's clothing apart from her gloves, yet they're as central to her style as her handbag,' says Genevieve James, who runs the eponymous glove-making label established by her mother Cornelia James in the 1940s.

'My mother was a Jewish refugee from Austria,' James continues, 'and the story goes that she escaped to England with her suitcase of leathers and nothing else.' James created gloves in a vibrant array of hues that women used to cheer up their outfits; '*Vogue* called her "the colour queen of England",' says James.

Her association with royalty began in 1947, when she was asked to create gloves for Princess Elizabeth's honeymoon trousseau. After that, Cornelia James gloves became a linchpin of the future monarch's style and, in 1979, the business was granted a Royal Warrant.

In the 1940s and '50s, gloves were part of the everyday uniform of British women – 'If you're wearing a hat, you must wear gloves,' confirms James – but as time has passed, the Queen has come to represent a bygone era of style standards.

'She wears them because they are part of her iconic style,' muses James, 'but she's also meeting a lot of people and shaking a lot of hands, so they add protection.' When the Queen visited Nigeria in 1956, she preceded Princess Diana by making a powerful gesture through the simple act of a handshake with leprosy sufferers. Even though she was wearing gloves, her willingness to break taboos helped to begin easing centuries of prejudice.

Although James creates gloves in a glamorous array of fabrics, many of which appear in films and TV shows such as *Bridgerton*, the monarch sticks to black, white and occasionally parchment gloves. She owns around 40 or 50 pairs, 'but often it's the older styles which come out again,' notes James.

For all her show business and socialite clients, James says that 'the one person who counts for me is the Queen. She's a great ambassador. There's this iconic vision of her in her black limousine with a white gloved hand at the window.'

BELOW In her customary white gloves, the Queen takes a photograph while visiting Tuvalu in the South Pacific, October 1982.

Queen Elizabeth II dons her favoured accessories – hat, gloves and handbag, plus a triple string of pearls – during a State Visit to Mexico in 1975.

THE HATS

A hat is more than the cherry on the cake of the Queen's look. It is the anchor of the whole thing. Whether she is watching a welcoming ceremony in baking heat, enjoying a day at Royal Ascot or opening a hospital, a hat has become a stand-in crown for the sovereign, making her visible to as many people as possible.

'People want to see me,' the Queen has said by way of explanation for her meticulous approach to millinery. In 2007, she wrote that she 'must be almost the only person who wears hats constantly' in a letter to one of her favourite milliners, Philip Somerville.

While her headwear must be eye-catching and bold, large brims or details that obscure her face are no-nos. 'The reason she always wears a hat is to stand out in the crowd,' another favourite milliner, Frederick Fox, once said. He also expressed his frustration that Her Majesty would wear his hats pushed back on her head, which helped her to be seen.

Like gloves, hats were a non-negotiable aspect of Elizabeth's wardrobe growing up in a time when smart women

never left the house without one. Over time, widespread daily wearing of hats has diminished, but the monarch has continued her dedication to them, making them an indispensable part of her uniform.

Elizabeth II has worked with many milliners over the years and has never been afraid to experiment, but some of her most exciting styles

ABOVE The Queen wearing a petal-strewn hat in pastel shades that coordinates perfectly with her dress and coat during a visit to Northern Ireland in July 1966.

were created by Simone Mirman, a French milliner who trained under the pioneering couturière Elsa Schiaparelli, famed for her surreal and shocking creations, before moving to London with her husband Serge, who sold Christian Dior in the UK for the first time.

'My mother came to the UK not speaking a word of English,' remembers Mirman's daughter Sophie. 'She started making hats for Princess Margaret, who pushed her to explore making hats in different materials and fabrics. She was really adventurous in her style of hat. It was Princess Margaret who introduced my mother to the Queen.'

Mirman worked with Norman Hartnell, fashioning hats to match his creations for the monarch. Two or three options would be offered to the Queen for each outfit, presenting 'quite a creative challenge'. The monarch and her milliner would 'always converse in French', an excellent opportunity for Elizabeth II to keep up her impressive language skills.

'My mother would never let a client walk out of her salon with a hat which she didn't feel suited her. She would take into account the shape of the face, the outfit they were wearing,' says Sophie. 'For the Queen it would have to suit her. My mother said the Queen was very easy to make hats for because she had such an extraordinary head for hats. The wonderful challenge that my mother had was that everything had to be unique, the colours had to be strong and there was always a nod to the event that the Queen was going to.'

From turbans ('My mother was also known as the queen of turbans. The Queen had a great head for turbans,' Sophie comments) to silk head scarves or hats with delicate cascades of silk flowers, Mirman's many creations for the sovereign are endlessly enchanting.

The Chelsea Flower Show hairnet

One of the very few daytime events to which the Queen doesn't wear a hat is the Chelsea Flower Show. Between the early 1970s and the early 2010s, she often donned a black hairnet adorned with bows or small flowers instead, but more recently has gone without a head covering entirely. The reason for this remains a mystery.

ABOVE The Queen wearing a black bow-adorned hairnet at Chelsea Flower Show, London, May 1996.

Spotlight on Rachel Trevor-Morgan, the Queen's favourite milliner

'The Queen has probably worn more hats than anyone else, so to have her wearing my hats is an extraordinary thing. Nowadays she has a more set style, but she looks incredible and it works for her at this point in her life. I like the matchy-matchy thing that she does; it's so smart and chic. Often I take inspiration from the beautiful print on her dresses, which you don't always see when she's out because she often has a coat on, but you see flashes of it. They might be beautiful flowers or wispy, feathery prints, so you try and tie those together.

'The Queen enjoys fashion but it's a working outfit for her, so she doesn't want brims that are too big if she's getting in and out of cars; there are practical things to take into consideration. It also needs to be comfortable – you don't want a hat that you need to be worrying about.

'For a lot of the hats, it's just the beautiful colourways that I love. When she arrived at Balmoral for her summer break in 2021, she was wearing a pink outfit designed by Stewart Parvin with one of my hats. To see her on the cover of *Hello!* magazine that week looking radiant and beautiful in those colours was wonderful.'

RIGHT Queen Elizabeth II on her arrival at Balmoral as she takes up summer residence at the Castle, August 2021.

Four of the Queen's most remarkable hats

The 'Smartie' hat

Marie O'Regan designed more than
200 hats for the Queen, but the most
famous has to be the 'Smartie' hat,
a witty creation worn in Budapest in
1993 and made to match an outfit by
Ian Thomas. You cannot help but smile
when you see this flamboyant outfit,
and the Queen is unmissable.

The 'spaghetti' hat

On tour in Germany in May 1965, the
Queen debuted a diplomatically orange
Simone Mirman creation consisting of
an artful jumble of noodle-like strands –
it was dubbed the 'spaghetti' hat and is
a perfect example of the playful pieces
loved by the monarch around this time.

The back-to-front hat

'She never says she doesn't like something. She may say, "Oh, Philip doesn't like that",' Frederick Fox once said. The Duke of Edinburgh's opinion was always indispensable – when Angela Kelly suggested that the hat the monarch was to wear to the closing ceremony of the Commonwealth Games in Malaysia in 1998 would look better worn backwards, the Queen accepted her advice after consulting her husband, who 'always tells her the truth'.

The tam o'shanter

Elizabeth II paid tribute to Scottish hat tradition with this rich green tam o'shanter hat in 1980. Named after the eponymous hero of a Robert Burns poem, the style can also be called a Balmoral bonnet, so is a fitting reference to the sovereign's home north of the border. She wore this stylish design meeting with soldiers from the Royal Marines – her millinery choice complemented their berets nicely.

THE QUEEN'S jewels

'On gala evening at Covent Garden, staged to entertain visiting heads of state, the clothes of the English ladies would be compared unfavourably to those made in Paris and worn by the visitors,' Hardy Amies once wrote. 'It was always the British, however, who wore the most important jewellery. As a wag once put it (it might have been me): "The frogs may have the frocks, but we've got the rocks." '

And no one has a more spectacular selection of rocks than the Queen, for whom precious jewellery has been a part of her life since childhood. In a tradition started by Queen Victoria, the little Princess would be given pearls by King George V, or 'Grandpapa England' as she knew him, every birthday.

George V's wife Queen Mary, renowned for her vast jewellery collection and love for piling on as many exceptional pieces as possible so that her dresses were often hidden beneath a collage of jewels, cannot have failed to instil an appreciation for the beauty of gemstones and the artistry of jewellery in her granddaughter. 'The Queen wears a tiara with insouciance,' noted Hardy Amies. 'The Queen's dresser was to tell me on a later occasion that the Queen was the only person who could put on a tiara going downstairs.' This ease at wearing some of the world's most precious stones can only have come from a rare familiarity with these creations fostered from an early age.

In the documentary *Royal Family*, which aired in 1969 and is now banned from broadcast, there is one scene that shows the Queen examining the Timur ruby necklace. 'This is a fascinating necklace,' she says. 'One ought to get a dress designed especially so that one can wear it. The history is very fascinating. It belonged to the kings of Persia and Mogul emperors and came down to Queen Victoria who was sent it from India. It would be nice if one could go on wearing it.' It's a snapshot that leaves us in no doubt about the expertise the Queen has developed when it comes to her jewellery stash.

But Elizabeth II has also refreshed the way that the royal jewellery collection is worn, in step with the monarchy's evolving relationship with the public and the changing standards of society. 'Queen Elizabeth II has pushed back the tide of jewels and wears them as accoutrements of majesty when the occasion requires; for official dinners, royal tours, the State Opening of Parliament,' wrote Suzy Menkes in her book *The Royal Jewels*. 'The collapse of formal society, which was never rebuilt after the war, and the erosion of aristocratic private life by post-war inflation, combined to make the Queen a bejewelled island from whom the rest of society receded,' she added.

Early in the Queen's reign, there were many occasions when a full set of dazzling jewels were required and it perhaps felt more appropriate to be quintessentially regal, showing off her incredible inheritance from Queen Mary, who died in 1953, and the generous gifts she had received for her wedding and coronation. 'Like any girl, the Queen looks her best with her tiara on, her full regalia,' Norman Hartnell observed.

Seven decades later, we undoubtedly still appreciate a dazzling jewellery moment, but the Queen has honed her way of wearing jewellery. She prefers just one necklace at a time (usually a string of pearls by day), a delicate pair of earrings (again, usually pearls or diamonds) and a carefully chosen brooch. Each morning, Angela Kelly, who is in charge of the Queen's jewels as well as her wardrobe, will lay out a choice for the sovereign to pick from on a tray that once belonged to Queen Mary.

Elizabeth II and her family recognize the emotion that can be woven through jewellery, too. She has had brooches made for her mother and received thoughtful gifts from her husband that have updated the many pieces that date back to the Victorian era. She has also loaned items to the other women in the Royal family, allowing them to write a new chapter in the incredible history of these jewels.

This jewellery approach is a mere whisper compared to the ostentation of her grandmother, but the Queen has found a way that melds her own modest personal style with the splendour of the unique collection that is locked away in the vaults of Buckingham Palace.

THE QUEEN'S MOST IMPORTANT JEWELS

The Girls of Great Britain and Ireland tiara

This delicate tiara is said to be the Queen's favourite. It is certainly one of her most regularly worn, which may have something to do with it being the lightest in her huge collection. Although many of her jewels can be traced back to Queen Mary, the story behind this diadem means that Her Majesty still refers to this one as 'Granny's tiara'. The piece takes its name from the committee of women, headed by Lady Eva Greville, who clubbed together to buy it as a wedding gift for Mary in 1893. Featuring festoon and fleur-de-lys motifs, many have observed that the jewels create the appearance of a line of girls dancing hand in hand. Queen Mary gave the tiara to Elizabeth as a wedding gift and she's worn it regularly ever since.

The Greville chandelier earrings

Some of the Royal family's most spectacular pieces of jewellery are part of a generous bequest left to the Queen Mother by Dame Margaret Greville 'with all my loving thoughts' to the woman who was said to be like the daughter she never had. Dame Margaret was a jewellery superfan; a client of Cartier and Boucheron, she travelled the world adding to her treasure trove. The chandelier earrings, which Princess Elizabeth received as a wedding present from her mother, were designed by Cartier and are described by the Royal Collection Trust as incorporating 'a lexicon of modern diamond cuts, including half-moon, trapeze, square, baguette, baton and emerald'.

The 'spare' diamond festoon necklace

In 1950, King George VI decided to put an inheritance of over 200 diamonds to good use, commissioning a triple-strand festoon necklace for his daughter and heir. The design is especially sentimental to the Queen, for whom it has become a favourite.

The Dorset bow brooch

This charming bow brooch was a gift from the people of Dorset to Princess Mary in 1893. It's thought that its makers Carrington & Co. may have been inspired by a similar brooch belonging to the trendsetting Empress Eugénie of France. Another of Mary's wedding gifts to Elizabeth, it's one of the few pieces that the Queen has worn for both day and evening. It was chosen for Prince Charles's christening and Princess Anne's first wedding.

Queen Alexandra's Kokoshnik tiara

When the Prince and Princess of Wales, later King Edward VII and Queen Alexandra, celebrated their silver wedding anniversary in 1888, a committee of women formed with the intention of buying a gift for Alexandra. She knew exactly what she wanted: a diamond fringe tiara like the one owned by her

sister Empress Marie Feodorovna of Russia. The style emulated the traditional Russian 'kokoshnik' headdress. Created by Garrard, each of the diamonds in the tiara's 61 bars matches perfectly.

BELOW Queen Elizabeth II wears Queen Alexandra's Kokoshnik tiara with her triple-strand diamond festoon necklace, commissioned by George VI, in Mexico, 1975.

'Granny's chips'

There are few people on the planet who could casually refer to two of the world's most impressive diamonds as 'Granny's chips', but the Queen is one of them. The nickname for the 94.4-carat Cullinan III and 63.6-carat Cullian IV diamonds was revealed when the monarch visited Asscher's, the jewellers who had cut the original Cullinan diamond, the largest gem-quality rough diamond ever found, in 1958. During the visit, she wore 'Granny's chips' and removed the brooch to allow Louis Asscher to take a closer look, a gesture that reportedly reduced him to tears.

Discovered in South Africa in 1905 and named after the mine's chairman Thomas Cullinan, the two largest diamonds cut from the stone – including the 'Star of Africa' – now form part of the Crown Jewels, while the seven other diamonds are owned by the Queen. She inherited them from Queen Mary, who was given them as a gift from the government of South Africa in 1910. Mary was renowned for her creative styling of this unique diamond collection, wearing them in all manner of combinations over the years.

This is one of the Queen's grandest-looking brooches and not one that has been worn regularly. Though what piece could have been more appropriate for Elizabeth II to wear on the occasion of her 2012 Diamond Jubilee than two of the most magnificent diamonds in the world?

The Burmese Ruby tiara

This tiara is a blend of two of the most magnificent wedding gifts received by Princess Elizabeth; the diamond tiara she chose from Cartier, courtesy of the Nizam of Hyderabad, and 96 glimmering rubies from the people of Burma, given, according to Garrard, as 'a symbolic gesture, as rubies in Burmese culture protect from illness and evil, in this case to protect the wearer from the 96 diseases that can afflict humans.'

In 1973, the jeweller combined the diamonds and rubies from these two gifts into a glittering new tiara, incorporating a Tudor rose motif. The tiara, and the story behind it, went viral in 2019 when the Queen wore it to a State Banquet attended by Donald Trump. Had Her Majesty donned the tiara in the hope that those rubies would protect her from the controversial US President? Of course, the Queen would never deign to make a jewellery decision that was anything less than supremely diplomatic.

OPPOSITE Very fittingly, Queen Elizabeth II chose to wear 'Granny's chips', or the Cullinan III and IV diamond brooch, to a 2012 Service of Thanksgiving to celebrate her Diamond Jubilee.

RIGHT The Queen wears her Burmese Ruby tiara with the Crown Ruby necklace at a State Banquet for US President Donald Trump, 2019.

The Cambridge
pearl drop brooch

Before the current Duchess of Cambridge came Augusta, wife to Prince Adolphus, the tenth child of King George III. She accumulated numerous pieces of jewellery that were eventually inherited by her granddaughter Queen Mary.

Like so many of Elizabeth II's heirloom pieces of jewellery, the pearl drop brooch, thought to have been made by Garrard in the mid-19th century, has stood the test of time, looking as stylish pinned to Her Majesty's shoulder now as it did fastened at Augusta's neck almost 200 years ago.

The State Diadem

Anyone who has ever posted a letter in the UK will be familiar with the State Diadem, which the Queen wears in the profile portrait seen on Royal Mail stamps. This magnificent crown is set with 1,333 diamonds forming the national emblems of England, Scotland and Ireland, and is usually only seen at the State Opening of Parliament or in portraits.

The diadem was originally crafted by Rundell's as part of an order that King George IV would wear at his coronation, a celebration described as a 'superbly extravagant pageant'. The dazzling design has since been reserved for reigning queens or queen consorts.

The Edinburgh
wedding bracelet

Prince Philip had quite the family jewellery vault to contend with when he married Princess Elizabeth in 1947, and it might have been understandable if he hadn't bothered to compete with Queen Mary's staggering bounty of diamonds. Instead, he made use of the diamonds from a tiara that had been given to his mother, Princess Alice, by her aunt and uncle Tsar Nicholas II and Tsarina Alexandra of Russia and which she had somehow managed to save throughout the upheaval she experienced, from exile to mental breakdown.

Philip used some stones to create an engagement ring and others for an Art Deco-style bracelet; he designed the glittering pieces for his bride that the jewellers Philip Antrobus then made for him. The bracelet has become a particularly special part of Elizabeth II's collection.

The Nizam of
Hyderabad necklace

The Nizam of Hyderabad, leader of a region of central India, was one of the richest men in the world when Elizabeth married in 1947. He instructed her to choose any gifts she liked from Cartier. She opted for a tiara and this necklace, which Hugh Roberts, former director of the Royal Collection and author of *The Queen's Diamonds*, describes as having a 'pavé-set centre with detachable double-drop pendant incorporating 13 emerald-cut diamonds and a pear-shaped drop; the chain of 38 brilliant-cut open-back collets with an elongated oval brilliant-set snap'.

The necklace, originally created in 1935, was a favourite of the Queen's early in her reign. In recent years, it has gained popularity with a new generation, having been borrowed by the Duchess of Cambridge.

ABOVE LEFT The Queen wearing the historic Cambridge pearl drop brooch on a walkabout during the New Zealand leg of her Silver Jubilee Tour, 1977.

The Queen wears the State Diadem and the Nizam of Hyderabad necklace with the Edinburgh wedding bracelet for this formal portrait in 1955.

The Brazilian parure

This may be the Queen's most spectacular set of jewels. Now comprising a tiara, necklace, bracelet and earrings, the Brazilian parure has its origins in a gift of aquamarines given to Elizabeth II by the people of Brazil in 1953 to mark her coronation and made into a necklace and earrings. Over the years, more of the dazzling blue gems have been added to the collection and the pieces reworked in various guises. The Queen is often careful to honour her guests by wearing jewels that have been gifted by them or their countries, so it was only natural that she would wear the aquamarine parure for state banquets with the presidents of Brazil in 1976 and 1997.

The Grand Duchess Vladimir tiara

The magnificent Grand Duchess Vladimir is one of the Queen's most versatile tiaras – it can be worn 'widowed' without pendant gems or with emeralds or pearls hanging from its interlocking diamond loops.

When Duchess Marie of Mecklenburg-Schwerin, a German Princess, married Grand Duke Vladimir Alexandrovich of Russia in 1874, the favoured jeweller of the Russian Imperial Court, Bolin, created the spectacular tiara for the new Grand Duchess.

During the Russian Revolution in 1917, the Grand Duchess fled her home leaving her jewels locked

in a safe. They were eventually smuggled to London in an elaborate operation orchestrated by her son Boris and an art dealer friend. However, the tiara was damaged on arrival, and although the Grand Duchess escaped, she died soon after reaching safety in Europe. Her daughter Elena inherited the tiara and in 1921 sold it to Queen Mary, who had the headpiece repaired and updated to be able to display emeralds as well as pearls. It was one of the many pieces that Elizabeth II inherited and has continued to showcase over the decades.

The Duchess of Gloucester's pendant earrings

These earrings were originally part of a collection belonging to Princess Mary, Duchess of Gloucester and Edinburgh, the 11th of King George III's 15 children and the longest-surviving of her siblings. She bequeathed the diamond and

pearl jewels to her niece, Princess Mary Adelaide, Duchess of Teck, who later left them to her own daughter, who went on to become Queen Mary. In January 1947, Mary gave the top part of the earrings to Princess Elizabeth, who wore them on her wedding day. By the time Elizabeth inherited the lower parts of the earrings in 1953, a new diamond stud top section had been created.

Queen Victoria's Golden Jubilee necklace

When Queen Victoria celebrated her Golden Jubilee in 1887, a committee of influential women formed to raise money for a gift to mark the occasion. They decided to erect a statue of Prince Albert in Windsor Great Park, but there were funds left over. A wrangle ensued, with disagreements first about how the money should be spent, and once a piece of jewellery was decided upon, exactly what it should be – Victoria even threatened to remodel the gift if she didn't like it.

Ultimately, a magnificent pearl and diamond necklace was commissioned from Carrington & Co. and presented to Queen Victoria in 1888. The design is described by Hugh Roberts as

'eight graduated brilliant-set trefoil links, 12 smaller links and a snap, each centred by a graduated pearl, the crowned quatrefoil centre with pearl drop'. The necklace has become a favourite of the Queen's for state events.

ABOVE LEFT The Queen wears the Grand Duchess Vladimir tiara in its emerald setting for a gala ballet performance at the Paris Opera House, 1957.

ABOVE Wearing the Duchess of Gloucester's pendant earrings with Queen Victoria's Golden Jubilee necklace and The Girls of Great Britain and Ireland tiara, 1961.

OPPOSITE The Brazilian parure worn by the Queen at a State Banquet at Buckingham Palace to honour President Cardoso of Brazil in 1997.

The Andrew Grima brooch

The Andrew Grima brooch is a rare gem in the Queen's jewellery box; it is not an inherited piece or a lavish gift from a foreign land, but was given to her by her husband in 1966. Created by the eponymous jeweller, renowned for his forward-thinking approach, it is more modern-looking than many of the sovereign's other brooches, with its arrangement of abstract rubies and diamonds set in rays of gold. Elizabeth II has used the brooch to emphasize her dedication to Prince Philip, wearing it in photographs to mark their 70th wedding anniversary and for her first public engagement following his death.

The Richmond brooch

When Prince George married Princess Mary of Teck, later Queen Mary, in 1893, the people of Richmond gave her this intricate diamond and pearl brooch, a particularly touching gift, as her family has lived at White Lodge in Richmond Park for many years. It has become one of the Queen's best-loved brooches and has been pinned to her shoulder on the happiest and saddest of occasions; she wore it at the wedding of Prince Harry and Meghan Markle in 2018 but also at the funeral of Prince Philip in April 2021.

ABOVE Queen Elizabeth II wears the Richmond brooch to the funeral of Prince Philip at St George's Chapel, Windsor Castle, April 2021.

The New Zealand silver fern brooch

The Queen spent the Christmas of 1953 in New Zealand, two months into her six-month Commonwealth tour. On Christmas Day, Lady Allum, wife of the Mayor of Auckland, gave the sovereign a diamond and platinum brooch that paid tribute to the country's silver fern symbol, which has particular resonance in Maori culture. Ever since, it has been worn on any New Zealand-related engagement. The Duchess of Cambridge also borrowed the gift when she visited the islands in 2014. There is now a portrait of the Queen at Government House in Wellington that depicts her wearing the important brooch.

ABOVE Queen Elizabeth II wears her diamond and platinum silver fern brooch in New Zealand, 1954.

OPPOSITE The Queen in May 2021, sporting the Andrew Grima brooch given to her by the Duke of Edinburgh.

OPPOSITE The Queen
and Princess Anne on a
visit to Turkey in 1971.

THE QUEEN as muse

'I think the reason for the Queen having become such a towering
fashion icon is the feeling that she never wore anything because
she wanted to set a trend,' says Ian Griffiths, creative director of
Max Mara. 'In fact, the very use of the words "Queen" and "trend"
in the same sentence seems ridiculous – jarring even.'

Fashion may set the tone for what we wear, influencing us to swap from midi to maxi skirts or navy to burgundy from one season to the next, but those who are most admired in the world of style would never succumb to such influences. And there is no one quite like Elizabeth II for being utterly unlikely to be seen tapping into a whim.

'The Queen is the most stylish and original woman in the world; she is not like anyone else,' confirms former *Harper's Bazaar* editor-in-chief Justine Picardie. 'Fashion is about making people look like each other, but the Queen embodies the quote that is always attributed to Coco Chanel; "Fashion fades, style is eternal".'

To be so well known for such a singular look is no mean feat. Stewart Parvin describes the delicate tightrope between consistency and transformation that Elizabeth II's wardrobe must walk: 'The Queen has always had a look,

but it has hugely evolved over the years. At one point in the 1960s she was wearing shorter skirts and sleeveless dresses. You think the Queen's style doesn't change, but actually it does change an awful lot.'

The Queen and her courtiers are unlikely to ever want us to think only about her outfits or to breathlessly anticipate her next fashion statement – she's very far from being a mere clothes horse, after all. But if there's anyone to prove how inextricably linked our clothing choices are with the way the world perceives us – and how we can influence the world's view of us – then it's Elizabeth II.

'For somebody of her age to still be considering what she wears in such a careful way shows that she's so aware of the importance of it,' confirms Parvin. 'She's got a very definite sense of her own style, what works for her and what she likes,' adds milliner Rachel Trevor-Morgan.

As such, Her Majesty is revered by designers, and many of the best-known names in the industry have spoken of their respect for Elizabeth II. The late, famously acerbic Chanel designer Karl Lagerfeld had nothing but good things to say, commenting that, '[The Queen] is flawless. For this job, in our day, she is perfect.'

After a fashion reception in Italy in October 2000 attended by Her Majesty, Gianfranco Ferré said that, 'she is so perfect in the clothes she wears', while Rosita Missoni described her as 'so classy, so elegant'. And Miuccia Prada – a woman regarded as the epitome of excellent taste – called the Queen 'simply, one of the most elegant women in the world'.

Even if at times fashion critics have observed that the Queen's look is not exactly cutting edge, there has been a quiet admiration for her dedication to tradition. In 2002, *The Washington Post*'s Robin Givhan wrote that Her Majesty 'seems to revel in her frumpiness, which, of course, only makes it more splendid'.

Since Givhan made that statement, the fashion industry has reframed a certain kind of frumpiness as eccentric and cool, while Angela Kelly has stepped in to ensure the sovereign's outfits are sharper and sleeker than ever, so it's perhaps no surprise that in her nineties, there is barely a fashion season that goes by without some fashion label or another taking the Queen as its inspiration. And each one seems to hone in on a different aspect of her majestic look.

On 2 June 2016, the 63rd anniversary of the coronation, Gucci became the first brand to be allowed to stage a fashion show at Westminster Abbey, the setting for Elizabeth II's coronation. The Italian house's creative director, Alessandro Michele, who had set about transforming it with his vision of vintage-inflected eclecticism, revealed that the monarch was one of his greatest muses. 'The Queen is one of the most quirky people in the world,' he told *The New Yorker*, ahead of presenting a collection full of Queen-isms, from Balmoral-worthy kilts to ladylike handbags and matchy-matchy skirt suits.

It has often been cultural depictions of the Queen – rather than the woman herself – that kick-started the curiosity of creatives before they delved into her style archive. In 2011, the Italian designers Domenico Dolce and Stefano Gabbana cited Helen Mirren's Oscar-winning performance as the monarch in Stephen Frears' film *The Queen* as their starting point, telling the *Independent* that 'the scarves in particular' in their most recent collection were 'a clear reference to the Queen's style'.

Since Netflix launched its hit series *The Crown* in 2016, the nods to Elizabeth II have focused as much on the early regal looks recreated for Claire Foy, the actress who played her in the show's first two seasons, as the colour blocking for which she is so well known now. One of the most thoughtful examples of this was Erdem Moralioglu's spring/summer 2018 collection, which sprung from the designer's research in the Royal Collection at Windsor Castle and a particular fascination with the Queen's 1958 meeting with American jazz musician Duke Ellington in Leeds. Ellington wrote her a piece of music called 'The Queen's Suite' and 'she wrote him a note where she said, "I'll be listening",' Moralioglu told American *Vogue*.

The resulting show reimagined Queenly classics with a Harlem twist, spanning opulent brocade dresses, Argyle cardigans and jewelled satin gowns worn with long white gloves that looked remarkably similar to Norman Hartnell's designs of the era. And it felt as if the story had come full circle when the Duchess of Cambridge chose to wear a fitted tweed dress from this collection, honouring her grandmother-in-law's 1950s look.

Even young designers have found the sovereign's style a treasure trove of inspiration. 'There are many aspects of the Queen's style that I love, but it is particularly her use of colour that really resonates with me, as well as her ever-present small handbag, which constantly hangs from her arm,' said Shrimps founder Hannah Weiland, who designed her autumn/winter 2020 collection as an ode to the Royal family; a mishmash of references to the Queen,

PAGES 166 AND 167 Alessandro Michele's 2017 collection for Gucci Cruise, shown at the cloisters of Westminster Abbey in June 2016 (page 166), was inspired in part by Queen Elizabeth II's style, seen here on a visit to the Solomon Islands in 1982 (page 167).

BELOW AND OPPOSITE Erdem Moralioglu's spring/summer 2018 collection (below) took inspiration from the Queen's evening wear, including dresses such as this one (opposite), worn on a trip to Nigeria in 1956.

Princess Anne, Princess Diana and more. 'I love the continuity of her looks, her trademark pearls and how she always wears a hat to match,' Weiland continues, picking out the Queen's lime 90th birthday look as a favourite. 'The neon green particularly made her pearls pop.'

The following year, Ian Griffiths at Max Mara paid tribute to the Queen with his autumn/winter 2021–2022 show, basing his designs on Elizabeth II's off-duty ensembles. 'I think the Queen is the *ne plus ultra* of

authentic British style, and what I love about that style is that, despite any notions we might have about class divisions, it's a completely democratic look,' he explains. 'In lockdown, I wore my walking boots, waxed jacket, quilted gilet, Tattersall check shirt and tweed cap every day, and it struck me on our daily dog walks that I wasn't alone: just about everyone else was wearing variations on the same look. It looks good on anyone, but no one does it better than the Queen.'

Griffiths believes that 'the Queen looks best in off-duty mode', picking out visuals of 'her striding out wearing a mid-calf kilt, quilted jacket, stout boots with chunky hand-knitted socks, a headscarf and big sunglasses'. Why do these outfits resonate? 'She looks completely at ease in what she's wearing, unselfconscious and nonchalant,' he observes, 'and I've always thought that's the key to looking good. It's a look that says you're getting things done, it's practical, pragmatic and it just exudes glamour. I like to think that the woman I design for is as cool, confident and capable as the Queen.'

The Queen's one-time couturier Ian Thomas once said that, 'she is too intelligent a person to be infatuated by fashion or worry too much about it'. In today's context, it's a quote that might be perceived as doing fashion a disservice, but it's evident that Her Majesty cares greatly about design excellence (the Queen Elizabeth II Award for British Design is given to a young creative each year at London Fashion Week) in the thoughtful clothing decisions she is making well into the tenth decade of her life, which so often dazzle those who see them as soon as they are beamed around the world on social media or on news websites. She may not give trends a second thought, but as for infatuation, it's all of us who are infatuated by Queen Elizabeth II, the ultimate modern power dresser.

OPPOSITE ABOVE AND BELOW The Shrimps autumn/winter 2020 fashion show, designed by Hannah Weiland, paid homage to the Royal family's enduring sense of style, as seen opposite above in an outfit that playfully references the Queen's classic off-duty style staples – jodphurs and a tweed riding jacket (opposite below).

LEFT AND ABOVE At the Max Mara autumn/winter 2021–2022 show, shown at Milan Fashion Week, February 2021, Ian Griffiths paid tribute to the Queen's off-duty style of headscarf and tweeds (left), as seen at the Royal Windsor Horse Show, 1985 (above).

INDEX

PICTURE CREDITS

Page 1 Tim Graham Photo Library/Getty Images; 2 left Tim Graham Photo Library/Getty Images; 2 right Anwar Hussein/Getty Images; 3 Ullstein Bild Dtl/Getty Images; 4 Serge Lemoine/Getty Images; 5 left Lisa Sheridan/Hulton Archive/Getty Images; 5 right Tim Graham Photo Library/Getty Images; 6 Anwar Hussein/Getty Images; 7 M. McKeown/Hulton Archive/Getty Images; 8 Anwar Hussein/Getty Images; 9 Mark Cuthbert/Getty Images; 11 Getty Images; 12 Bob Thomas/Popperfoto/Getty Images; 14 Popperfoto/Getty Images; 16 Lisa Sheridan/Getty Images; 17 Dorothy Wilding/Getty Images; 18 PhotoQuest/Getty Images; 19 Hulton Archive/Getty Images; 20 Popperfoto/Getty Images; 22 Bert Hardy/Getty Images; 23 Getty Images; 24 Mirrorpix/Getty Images; 25 Mirrorpix/Getty Images; 26 Hulton Archive/Getty Images; 27 Keystone/Getty Images; 28 Print Collector/Getty Images; 29 Print Collector/Getty Images; 31 Keystone/Getty Images; 32 Hulton Archive/Getty Images; 33 Popperfoto/Getty Images; 34 Paul Popper/Popperfoto/Getty Images; 35 Hulton Archive/Getty Images; 36 Paul Popper/Popperfoto/Getty Images; 37 Reg Speller/Fox Photos/Getty Images; 38 Hulton Archive/Getty Images; 39 above Derek Berwin/Getty Images; 39 below Popperfoto/Getty Images; 40 Popperfoto/Getty Images; 43 AFP/Getty Images; 44 Hulton Archive/Getty Images; 45 above Keystone/Getty Images; 45 below Keystone-France/Getty Images; 46 Popperfoto/Getty Images; 47 Popperfoto/Getty Images; 48 above Rolls Press/Popperfoto/Getty Images; 48 below Anwar Hussein/Getty Images; 49 Anwar Hussein/Getty Images; 50 above Anwar Hussein/Getty Images; 50 below Tim Graham Photo Library/Getty Images; 51 Ian Stewart/Getty Images; 52 Chris Jackson/Getty Images; 53 above John Stilwell/Pool/Getty Images; 53 below Samir Hussein/Getty Images; 54 Max Mumby/Indigo/Getty Images; 56 Ray Bellisario/Popperfoto/Getty Images; 57 left Ray Bellisario/Popperfoto/Getty Images; 57 right Tim Graham Photo Library/Getty Images; 58 above Fox Photos/Getty Images; 58 below Tim Graham Photo Library/Getty Images; 59 Chris Jackson/Getty Images; 60 Central Press/Getty Images; 61 left Tim Graham Photo Library/Getty Images; 61 right Chris Jackson/Getty Images; 62 Dominic Lipinski/WPA Pool/Getty Images; 63 left Max Mumby/Indigo/Getty Images; 63 right Ray Bellisario/Popperfoto/Getty Images; 64 above and below Tim Graham Photo Library/Getty Images; 65 Tim Graham Photo Library/Getty Images; 66 above Carl Court/Pool/Getty Images; 66 below Hulton-Deutsch/CORBIS/Getty Images; 67 above Fox Photos/Getty Images; 67 below Aaron Chown/Getty Images; 68 left Mark Cuthbert/Getty Images; 68 right Tim Graham Photo Library/Getty Images; 69 Bentley Archive/Popperfoto//Getty Images; 70 Hulton Archive/Getty Images; 72 Derek Berwin/Fox Photos/Hulton Archive/Getty Images; 73 Popperfoto/Getty Images; 74 above Rolls Press/Popperfoto/Getty Images; 74 below Hulton Archive/Getty Images; 75 Rolls Press/Popperfoto/Getty Images; 76 Anwar Hussein/Getty Images; 77 Wally McNamee/CORBIS/Getty Images; 78 Tim Graham Photo Library/Getty Images; 79 below Jeff Overs/Getty Images; 79 above Anwar Hussein/Getty Images; 80 Fiona Hanson/AFP/Getty Images; 81 above Tim Graham Photo Library/Getty Images; 81 below Royal Collection via Tim Graham Royal Photos/Getty Images; 82 Chris Jackson/Getty Images; 83 Eddie Mulholland/WPA Pool/Getty Images; 84 Cameron Spencer/Getty Images; 85 Yui Mok/WPA Pool/Getty Images; 87 Serge Lemoine/Getty Images; 88 above Mirrorpix/Getty Images; 88 below Keystone-France/Getty Images; 89 Fox Photos/Getty Images; 90 Paul Popper/Popperfoto/Getty Images; 91 Anwar Hussein/Getty Images; 93 left Anwar Hussein/Getty; 93 right David Cairns/Getty Images; 94 left Jonathan Drake/Getty Images; 94 right Tim Graham Photo Library/Getty Images; 95 Georges De Keerle/Getty Images; 96 left Max Mumby/Indigo/Getty Images; 96 right Yui Mok/AFP/Getty Images; 97 Tim Graham Photo Library/Getty Images; 99 Keystone-France/Getty Images; 100 Bettmann/Getty Images; 101 above Central Press/Getty Images; 101 below Bettmann/Getty Images; 102 Bettmann/Getty Images; 104 Anwar Hussein/Getty Images; 105 left Max Mumby/Indigo/Getty Images; 105 above David Levenson/Getty Images; 106-7 Matt Dunham/WPA Pool/Getty Images; 109 Glyn Kirk/WPA Pool/Getty Images; 110–111 DZY/Getty Images; 112 Max Mumby/Indigo/Getty Images; 113 Keystone/Fox Photos/Hulton Archive/Getty Images; 114 left Chris Jackson/Getty Images; 114 right Popperfoto/Getty Images; 115 Chris Jackson/Getty Images; 116 left Zak Hussein/CORBIS/Getty Images; 116 right Keystone/Hulton Archive/Getty Images; 117 Tim Graham Photo Library/Getty Images; 118 Hulton Archive/Getty Images; 119 Tim Graham Photo Library/Getty Images; 120 Max Mumby/Indigo/Getty Images; 121 Tim Graham Photo Library/Getty Images; 122 Chris Jackson/Getty Images; 123 Andrew Meares/AFP/Getty Images; 124 above Oli Scarff/WPA/Getty Images; 124 below Tim Graham Photo Library/Getty Images; 125 Popperfoto/Getty Images; 126 Hulton Archive/Getty Images; 128 left and right Tim Graham Photo Library/Getty Images; 129 Tim Graham Photo Library/Getty Images; 130 left and right Tim Graham Photo Library/Getty Images; 131 Tim Graham Photo Library/Getty Images; 132 Andrew Milligan/WPA Pool/Getty Images; 133 Bob Thomas/Popperfoto/Getty Images; 134 Max Mumby/Indigo/Getty Images; 135 Anwar Hussein/Getty Images; 136 Bob Thomas/Popperfoto/Getty Images; 137 Central Press/Hulton Archive/Getty Images; 138 Serge Lemoine/Getty Images; 139 Ian Waldie/Getty Images; 141 Tim Graham Photo Library/Getty Images; 142 Max Mumby/Indigo/Getty Images; 143 Serge Lemoine/Getty Images; 145 Tim Graham Photo Library/Getty Images; 146 Serge Lemoine/Getty Images; 147 Ray Bellisario/Popperfoto/Getty Images; 148 Tim Graham Photo Library/Getty Images; 149 Jane Barlow/WPA Pool/Getty Images; 150 left Tim Graham Photo Library/Getty Images; 150 right André Lefebvre/Paris Match/Getty Images; 151 below left Serge Lemoine/Getty Images; 151 above right Tim Graham Photo Library; 153 Fox Photos/Hulton Archive/Getty Images; 155 Serge Lemoine/Getty Images; 156 Adam Jacobs/Getty Images; 157 Dominic Lipinski/WPA Pool/Getty Images; 158 Anwar Hussein/Getty Images; 159 Hulton Archive/Getty Images; 160 Tim Graham Picture Library/Getty Images; 161 above Paul Popper/Popperfoto/Getty Images; 161 below George Freston/Fox Photos/Hulton Archive/Getty Images; 162 above Yui Mok/WPA Pool/Getty Images; 162 below Fox Photos/Hulton Archive/Getty Images; 163 Steve Parsons/WPA Pool/Getty Images; 164 Paul Popper/Popperfoto/Getty Images; 166 Daniele Venturelli/Getty Images; 167 Tim Graham Photo Library/Getty Images; 168 Ullstein Bild/Getty Images; 169 Victor Virgile/Gamma-Rapho/Getty Images; 170 left Anwar Hussein/Getty Images; 170 right Victor Virgile/Gamma-Rapho/Getty Images; 171 left Daniele Venturelli/Getty Images; 171 right Tim Graham Photo Library/Getty Images; 176 Chris Jackson/Getty Images.

ACKNOWLEDGMENTS

I would like to thank everyone who has shared their stories of dressing the Queen: the experts and designers who so kindly offered their wisdom and thoughts and the authors who came before me, this book is infinitely better for your insights.

This book is brought to life by so many beautiful images taken by many photographers throughout Her Majesty's lifetime. I thank them for capturing these moments and I often wished I could have stepped into their shoes while I was writing.

I am hugely grateful to my agents Heather and Elly for their endless enthusiasm and support, and also to Annabel, Cindy, Toni and Leslie for bringing this book together and making it look so wonderful.

To my bosses and colleagues at *The Telegraph*, who have always been so supportive, thank you for giving me the time and space for this project – and, of course, for always being so fun to talk to about Royal fashion.

Thank you to my brilliant friends and family for all their kindness, especially my mum, who always knows the right thing to say.

And to Johnny and our son who started growing as I wrote this book – you're the best.